Resilie...

Endorsement by Governor Mike Huckabee

I was privileged to provide the Foreword for General Bob Dees' first book, *Resilient Warriors,* in 2011. I knew at the time that this book would be relevant and popular, as has been the case. While *Resilient Warriors* had natural appeal to military personnel, their families, and military caregivers; the book had unexpected appeal to the general populace and to academia. At Liberty University, thousands of students have used *Resilient Warriors* in their psychology (undergraduate) and counseling (graduate) curriculums. The same content has fueled a multitude of small groups, conferences, and training seminars, branded as "Resilience God Style." Such faith-based resilience is critically needed in America today.

Now Bob Dees gives us the *Resilience God Style* book, containing the same valuable *Resilient Warriors* content, yet updated to appeal to an even broader audience and to complement the Resilience God Style curriculum and video series. *Resilience God Style* is an invaluable, Biblically-based tool for preparing for the inevitable storms of life, weathering those storms, and bouncing back without getting stuck in the toxic emotions of guilt, false guilt, anger, and bitterness.

I highly recommend *Resilience God Style* as your pathway to readiness for whatever challenges you may face, and a roadmap to recovery when we have hit the hard concrete of life. Resilience truly is a critical life skill—*Resilience God Style* will help you master it.

Prior Endorsements on Behalf of *Resilient Warriors*

"America's heroes have been at war for more than a decade, selflessly defending our nation. They are the brightest and bravest of their generation. General Bob Dees knows the dangers they have faced, the sacrifices they have made and the challenges confronting their loved ones. If you know a veteran of a long ordeal, *Resilient Warriors* is a 'must read' for them—and for you."

~ Lt. Col. Oliver L. North, USMC, Retired
Host of War Stories on FOX News and author of the "American Heroes" book series

"A must read book for every leader and care-giver intent on providing help and hope to those recovering from combat trauma or any painful, life-changing event. With extensive research and com- passionate observations, this resource offers valuable insights to veterans, past and present, who continue to navigate their way back home to normalcy. The spiritual principles of resilience presented in this book will help the reader manage the most difficult traumatic event in their life with increased confidence and the assurance of restoration. I highly recommend this book to every military chaplain in the critical pastoral care they daily provide to our veterans and their families."

~ Douglas L. Carver, Chaplain Major General, United States Army, Retired

"When life is not the way it is supposed to be...When you hit the wall and feel like you can't go on... Every life is filled with moments of crisis, loss & trauma. *Resilient Warriors* takes its readers to a safe place and profound insights, offering hope on the healing journey--a valuable resource for each of us, providing insightful coaching around the critical psychological and spiritual quality of resilience. General Bob Dees is a Resilient Warrior and Leader himself, well qualified to inspire and mentor us around this essential characteristic for individuals, leaders, and organizations. I look forward to *Resilient Leaders* and *Resilient Nations*, equally relevant parts of this significant *Resilience Trilogy*.

~ Dr. Tim Clinton, Ed.D., President, American Assn of Christian Counselors

Author of *The Bible for Hope and The Popular Encyclopedia of Christian Counseling*

"'*To really live you must almost die. To those who fight for it, life has a meaning the protected will never know.*' A very short but powerful phrase I first saw in a Special Forces team house in Vietnam, but it quickly became a reality in my life and put into words a truth about life...a meaning to life that would guide, encourage, and provide 'bounce' for me as I battled to come 'Home' from the war.

"War teaches many harsh lessons about life....about death...but, unfortunately, for too many of us those lessons remain locked away in our hearts and minds...buried deep beneath fear, guilt, anger, or pain and cannot provide the meaning, the wisdom, the resiliency, the 'bounce' needed to truly "Come home" from the war and battles of life. "General Dees is a man of war, but more importantly a man who has the gift of putting into words the unspoken thoughts that are hidden in the hearts of our nation's warriors. His words of wisdom and spiritual truth will provide for all warriors the ability to 'bounce back' from the battles and challenges each of us face and derive a meaning to life that others will never know."

~ Gary Beikirch, Medal of Honor, Vietnam

"As a family financial expert, mother of seven and military spouse, I've learned how to bounce back when life throws a curve ball. *Resilient Warriors* helps families, warriors and leaders have the all-important bounce. This series comprehensively looks at a tried-in-the-trenches means of achieving resilience. I appreciate General Bob Dees' compassionate Biblical wisdom on this topic, and the pastoral approach he brings to areas in our lives in need of timely attention. This practical resource also incorporates the applicable disciplines of physiology and psychology that will help any warrior, leader, organization or family live an above average life."

~ Ellie Kay, America's Family Financial Expert®, ABC News Financial expert
Author of 14 books including *Heroes at Home: Hope and Help for American Military Families*

Resilience God Style

Major General Robert F. Dees
US Army, Retired

www.ResilienceGodStyle.com

Creative Team Publishing
Ft. Worth, Texas

The *Resilience God Style Study Guide* is a separate publication, ISBN 978-0-9979519-3-6, which comprehensively addresses all chapters of *Resilience God Style* (1-10), providing additional content in an expanded study guide format. *Resilience God Style* and the *Resilience God Style Study Guide* also map directly to the *Resilience God Style Video Series*, and provide supporting content for the *Resilience God Style Training Game*.

SCRIPTURE REFERENCES:
All scripture quotations, unless otherwise indicated, are taken from the New American Standard Bible, Copyright © 1960, 1962, 1963, 1968, 1971, 1972, 1973, 1975, 1977, 1995 by The Lockman Foundation. Used by permission. (http://www.Lockman.org)
Scripture quotations marked "NKJV™" are taken from the New King James Version. Copyright © 1982 by Thomas Nelson, Inc. Used by permission. All rights reserved.
Scripture quotations marked (NIV) are taken from the Holy Bible, New International Version®, NIV®. Copyright © 1973, 1978, 1984, 2011 by Biblica, Inc. Used by permission of Zondervan. All rights reserved worldwide. http://www.zondervan.com.
The "NIV" and "New International Version" are trademarks registered in the United States Patent and Trademark Office by Biblica, Inc.™
Scripture quotations marked (NLT) are taken from the Holy Bible, New Living Translation, copyright © 1996, 2004, 2007. Used by permission of Tyndale House Publishers, Inc., Carol Stream, Illinois 60188. All rights reserved.

DISCLAIMERS:
This book is not a substitute for appropriate medical or psychological care for those experiencing significant emotional pain or whose ability to function at home, school, or work is impaired. Chronic or extreme stress may cause a wide assortment of physical and psychological problems. Some may require evaluation and treatment by medical   or mental health professionals. When in doubt, seek advice from a professional. You must not rely on the information in this book as an alternative to medical advice from your doctor or other professional healthcare provider. If you have any specific questions about any medical matter you should consult your doctor or other professional healthcare provider. If you think you may be suffering from any medical condition you should seek immediate medical attention. You should never delay seeking medical advice, disregard medical advice, or discontinue medical treatment because of information in this book.

During the process of constructing this book, due diligence has been undertaken to obtain all proper copyright permissions. If it comes to our attention that any citations are missing, they will be readily provided at http://www.ResilienceGodStyle.com.

ISBN: 978-0-9979519-2-9

PUBLISHED BY CREATIVE TEAM PUBLISHING
www.CreativeTeamPublishing.com
Ft. Worth, Texas
Printed in the United States of America

Resilience God Style

Major General Robert F. Dees
US Army, Retired

www.ResilienceGodStyle.com

Table of Contents

Table of Contents

Table of Contents

Table of Contents

Table of Contents

Table of Contents

Table of Contents

Foreword
Resilience God Style

(formerly *Resilient Warriors*, 2011)

Governor Mike Huckabee

Bob Dees is a "Christian General," just as leaders like Robert E. Lee, George A. Marshall, Dwight D. Eisenhower, and so many others who have selflessly served in the cloth of our nation while acknowledging their strong faith. Having provided his talents and perspective several times for the FOX show, *Huckabee*, Bob has also been part of adding color and deep background commentary as a part of two of my trips to the Middle East where he has notable expertise from having served there. He continues to be a trusted adviser to me on military issues in my role as a commentator and author. Of recent, Bob has risen to national stature because of his pioneering work to help troops, veterans, and their families with the "hidden wounds of war" and the lasting effects of combat trauma. As well, he provided superb counsel and leadership as Dr. Ben Carson's National Security Advisor and Campaign Chairman in the 2016 Presidential Campaign Cycle.

While Bob, himself, would make no claims to greatness, the fact is he has led U.S. military forces around the globe, and led them well, in the good times and in the tough times. He has much to offer to individual warriors (that's all of us!), leaders (that's most of us!), and organizations that seek to cultivate resilience as insurance for the coming storms of life. As is consistent with Bob's approach to leadership, he believes that "reality is our friend." His first book in The Resilience Trilogy, now updated as *Resilience God Style*, is no exception: he speaks clearly and candidly about the relevance of individual spirituality and faith in achieving comprehensive fitness and resilience for the unavoidable and the inevitable, the very real "body slams" of life.

I cannot think of a more relevant topic in today's world than "How to Bounce Back." General Dees combines the pervasive effects of national and global issues such as the economy, national security, energy, healthcare, and erosion of fundamental values with the ever-present personal issues such as employment, health, relationships, and ultimate purpose and meaning, to develop an engaging and powerful spiritual roadmap for surviving and thriving in the Before, During, and After phases of the storms of life. I know I will personally benefit from the inspiring stories and the practical precepts found in *Resilience God Style*. It's a goldmine of wisdom for each of us who seek to bounce our way through the small and large hiccups of life.

I know from my own life experience that "bouncing back" is essential. For instance, I lost my first political race in 1992, but bounced back in 1993 in a special election for Lieutenant Governor that led to my being Governor for almost eleven years and running for President. I didn't win the Presidency, but the effort opened doors in media that would never have happened without the path. Successes are simply different turns on the highway often road blocked by our disappointments. General Dees explains how getting knocked down is not getting knocked out.

As a final note, Bob's other books, *Resilient Leaders* and *Resilient Nations*, are equally compelling and significant, providing essential information and inspiration in helping individuals, leaders, and even nations become ready and resilient for any challenge they may face.

~ Mike Huckabee

This Book Is Dedicated to Resilient Warriors

- Those great veterans of times past who have preserved our freedoms and in their post-war years fought for a better future for all of us
- Those brave young military warriors of today who continue to go into harm's way on our behalf, many of whom "walk with a limp" with heads held high
- Those first responder warriors who stand daily watch over our citizens, our institutions, our future generations
- Those captains of industry, entrepreneurs, explorers, inventors, scientists, educators, civic leaders, and more who fight for a better tomorrow

And very importantly:

- Those family and friends of these warriors, who in themselves are warriors of the first order—
- Fighting through grief when their warriors get wounded, when their warriors pay the ultimate sacrifice
- Moving forward in faith when strength and courage fail

May these warriors continue to bounce back.

May they be resilient.

Where would we be without them?

Introduction
How High Will You Bounce?

This relevant question is frequently asked across all marketplaces of professional endeavor as well as the inner sanctums of our personal lives. In moments of introspection, uncertainty, or crisis have you asked yourself "How high do I bounce?" Or, looking into an uncertain future, anticipating the hard and concrete realities of overwhelming life situations, would you question, "How high *will* I bounce?"

During days of a crippling economy, persistent terror threats, terrifying natural disasters, wars and rumors of wars, it is natural to ask such questions. I certainly have asked them.

There are four primary analogies in the Scriptures: farming, fishing, athletics, and the military. A fifth over-arching analogy is God's Creation, illustrating key principles of resilience in the cycles of nature and the seasons. Springing from my own life experiences in the military, I will understandably lean heavily upon military analogy and the many military-related resilience principles found in the Scriptures. As well, the challenges of military life provide ample opportunities for observation of resilience under the toughest of conditions. Our nation's warriors well understand the challenges of bouncing back after repeated deployments, physical and mental wounds, or betrayal on the home front. They represent the "exoderm," the outer skin of our country, often wounded, cut, bleeding, and dying on our behalf.

As role models for warriors in every other marketplace and life endeavor, our nation's military men and women are inspiring and instructive as they meet the challenges of bouncing back.

Resilience God Style

Resilience God Style derives its primary content from *Resilient Warriors*, published in 2011. Since that time, the *Resilient Warriors* content (and the associated *Resilient Warriors Advanced Study Guide*) has proven relevant and popular across a wide range of venues, particularly as the primary texts for thousands of resilience students in psychology and counseling courses at Liberty University. *Resilient Warriors* content, now rebranded as "Resilience God Style," has also fueled hundreds of faith-based resilience presentations, training seminars, conferences, and small group studies.

The *Resilience God Style* book has a companion *Resilience God Style Study Guide* for personal and small group use, helping one personalize applications of the content. As well, this *Resilience God Style* book content is further amplified in the *Resilience God Style Video Series*, a nine-week study program for churches, small groups, and other organizations. Finally, the *Resilience God Style Training Game* is available as a fun, dynamic, and educational faith-based board game for home schoolers, Christian schools, and multi-generational family use.

The Need for Bounce

We use the term *resilience* to describe the process of bouncing back, as well as "upstream" actions to prepare for the "storms of life" and to weather these storms "until the destruction passes by…" (Psalm 57:1b) This resilience is a critical life skill for all of us, recognizing that adversity is an enduring reality and part of the "human condition." *Resilience God Style* uses Biblical truth as the primary source of enduring resilience principles and makes them available to "warriors" in every endeavor of life.

As I was falling twelve feet out of a British Lorry onto my back in Army Ranger School, many thoughts crossed my mind: "This is going to hurt! Will I break anything? Will I be able to bounce back?" Many of these same questions reemerged in parachute landing falls (PLFs in "Airborne" vernacular). They came again as I held my wife's hand when the Doctor informed us of our infant daughter's death. They were present when my helicopter in Macedonia was plummeting to the earth without power, and when the South Korean National Assembly asked for my removal because of my late night evacuation of a South Korean village in the impact radius of a suspected terrorist plot. The questions hounded me anew when I was unable to control events leading to the death of one of my troopers. They invaded once more during rare but painful incidents of disappointment and betrayal from over forty years of leadership in the military, business, and ministry. You, no doubt, get the point.

Most certainly you also have had plenty of opportunities to bounce. In addition to death and taxes, a veritable certainty of life is that we all get body slammed, kicked in the gut, blindsided, or simply overwhelmed with the crush of life's unrelenting demands.

Whether you are:
- A soldier on his third deployment to the Middle East (about the average) wondering whether the next Improvised Explosive Device (IED) has your name on it, or
- A businessman tottering on the edge of bankruptcy in a depressed economy, or
- A single mom wondering whether you will default on your home mortgage during the housing crisis, or
- A parent who is struggling to raise your kids among mounting teenage peer pressures, or
- A young man whose wife is suffering from cancer, or
- A single dad struggling with a debilitating disease like diabetes, or
- A military family fearful that "the doorbell might ring" and you will soon hear the words, "We regret to inform you that your loved one..."

For the vast majority of us, trial and tribulation are realities. Jesus reminded his disciples, "In the world you will have tribulation..." (John 16:33, NKJV) The question is not *if*, but *when*. Trauma is a reality. It is part of the human condition. We are all at war.

The reality is that as warriors we fight, we get wounded, and we bounce back to fight again—that is what warriors do. Resilience is a fundamental skill for warriors in every walk of life, a fundamental skill for each man, woman, and child on this planet.

> The reality is that as warriors we fight, we get wounded, and we bounce back to fight again—that is what warriors do.

Let me become more precise. I am talking about the nature and quality of bouncing back. Resilience is the ability for individuals, leaders, and organizations to take a hard hit and continue to pursue their mission, sort of like a National Football League (NFL) lineman who gets body slammed, takes a short breather on the sidelines, and then gets right back in the game. Resilience represents the ability to become better, not bitter; to bend but not break; to return to full function and potential after an internal or external shock; in short, to bounce back.

The term *resilience* is used across a variety of domains. The *Merriam-Webster's Collegiate® Dictionary* provides the following: *Resilience*: n.; "1: the capability of a strained body to recover its size and shape after deformation caused especially by compressive stress 2: an ability to recover from or adjust easily to misfortune or change." (Used by permission. From *Merriam-Webster's Collegiate® Dictionary* ©2011 by Merriam-Webster, Incorporated, www.Merriam-Webster.com).

Along similar lines, the Navy defines resilience as the "bounce factor" in their Combat Operational Stress Control (COSC) efforts.

The Army likewise uses the concept of bounce, such as a bouncing ball, in their resiliency training efforts associated with their Comprehensive Soldier Fitness (CSF) programs. We likewise use this metaphor of "bounce back" to describe resilience. Specifically, we contrast the bounce demonstrated by a tennis ball with the catastrophic impact and breakage which occurs when an egg splats on the ground. The egg metaphor is reminiscent of Humpty Dumpty who "...sat on a wall and had a great fall / and all the king's horses, and all the king's men / couldn't put Humpty together again." No doubt you, like me, would prefer the tennis ball experience.

Gratefully, we have strong resilience role models that inform and inspire us. Consider Joni Erickson Tada, "Rocky," numerous Prisoners of War, Twin Towers survivors, Congresswoman Gabrielle "Gabby" Giffords, the Warrior-King David among Biblical examples, or others who have beaten the odds, people who should have stayed flat on their face on the hard concrete of life but who, amazingly, miraculously, bounced back. Throughout *Resilience God Style* we will draw inspiration and example from a number of resilient warriors such as these.

The question, "How high will I bounce?" is relevant to us all. In other words, "How resilient will I be?" when the next heavy load forces me to my knees or lightening suddenly strikes my world? As with the frequent assertion made about leaders being both born and made, resilient people are also born (their genetic disposition) and made (their life experiences, education, and training). Certainly, God has dished out varying degrees of innate resilience to each of us. It is useful to be aware of our natural strengths and weaknesses regarding resilience. Even more relevant to each of us, however, is *how* to enhance our bounce factor in preparation for the next inevitable body slam of life. How do we proactively get "upstream" to develop resilience that allows us to resist, recover, and restore from future trauma?

Our journey together will explore the fine art of bouncing back. After covering the reality of life struggle and the nature of trauma, we will transition to positive ways to invest in resilience before, during, and after tragedy and trauma, trial and tribulation, occur. We will discuss the concepts of Posttraumatic Growth, and introduce a Resilience Life Cycle©, specifically discussing "Building Bounce" (before), "Weathering the Storm" (during), and "Bouncing Back" (after). Salting each chapter with stories and examples of resilience, we will be inspired by many "Profiles in Resilience," reminiscent of President John F. Kennedy's *Profiles in Courage*.

Beginning in 2011, I have had the privilege of informing and encouraging people from many diverse marketplaces with the theme, "Resilience God Style." I have seen business leaders and homemakers, pastors and chaplains, parents, mental health professionals and lay counselors, educators and students, athletes and coaches, military leaders and troops, military families, and veterans choose to invest in resilience to combat the inevitable traumas of life.

"How high will I bounce?" has proven to be a timely and important question in this rough and tumble world of ours. Perhaps a slight twist on the theme is even more important: "How do I bounce *high*?" or "How do I bounce *even higher* than before?" These questions beg for spiritual wisdom, recognizing that human strength alone is insufficient to surmount the array of challenges we potentially face. As in Zechariah 4:6, "Not by might nor by power, but by My Spirit says the Lord of hosts." In *Resilience God Style* we seek Biblical answers, principles, and techniques that will prepare us for the "cleverly disguised opportunities" that surely await us. We will learn how to "bounce high without getting stuck" and "bounce even higher" while helping others do the same.

Resilience possesses components which are both highly tangible (such as physical and mental) and less tangible (such as emotional, relational, and spiritual). While recognizing the importance of all dimensions of resilience, the spiritual arena is perhaps the one least understood and accepted in a culturally complex environment. As a result, we forthrightly integrate the "faith factor" into overall considerations of resilience.

Should we not now get everything in the fight, including faith, on behalf of our personal resilience? We will most certainly need it. Daunting and tragic statistics amply illustrate the need for resilience. Should we not all get everything in the fight, including faith, on behalf of the families, teams, and organizations we lead? They need every ounce of hope, courage, optimism, and resilience we can give them.

Consider a passage from the Bible's Resilience Chapter, 2 Corinthians 4:7-9 (underlining added for emphasis):

> [7] But we have this treasure in earthen vessels, so that the surpassing greatness of the power will be of God and not from ourselves. [8] We are <u>afflicted in every way</u>, but not crushed; <u>perplexed,</u> but not despairing; [9] <u>persecuted</u>, but not forsaken; <u>struck down</u>, but not destroyed.

These simple yet profound words define resilience well. Each of us are afflicted, perplexed, persecuted, and struck down often and in many ways. Yet, through faith and a relationship with Christ we are not destroyed and we are not broken beyond repair. Through Christ we become truly resilient. Through Christ we can "overwhelmingly conquer through Him who loved us." (Romans 8:37)

| Through Christ we become truly resilient. |

Resilience God Style comprehensively looks at the diverse means of achieving resilience, to include leveraging the full breadth and depth of Biblical wisdom on this topic, placing a pastoral approach alongside best practices of other applicable disciplines of physiology, psychology, and applicable arenas of medicine and science.

We begin.

1

Incoming!

Few words strike more fear into the heart of a warrior than does the warning, "Incoming!" Since the beginning of warfare, this cry has been used to signal approaching fire by enemy forces.

In modern times this alert generally refers to incoming artillery, rocket, or mortar fire, the insidious weapons of choice that precede their arrival with a haunting sound. The ordnance falls from above on vulnerable victims and impacts with overwhelming and often deadly force. In its wake it leaves residual fear about when and where the next fateful round will fall.

Many reading this will not soon forget or cease to re-experience your first mortar or artillery attack. It was a terrifying awareness of impending doom without a sure knowledge of the source, timing, or accuracy of the threat. Admittedly, today's technology affords the ability to rapidly suppress or eliminate indirect fire, but if you are the person on the ground receiving the first few rounds of incoming, you may be one shell burst away from a life changing injury or a fatal, final outcome.

"Incoming" is real, it is frightful, and it is often debilitating.

While not making light of the similar serious threats we all face, a little battlefield humor also helps along the way. Retired Army Major General Doug Carver, former Chief of Army Chaplains, tells a vignette from the early days of Operation Iraqi Freedom. When one of the early incoming SCUD alerts occurred, (Lightening! Lightening! Lightening!), Chaplain Carver relates that his assigned bunker was #13. Although a faithful man of God, he ran right past the empty Bunker #13 (perceived as being "unlucky") into the crush of over-flowing troops in Bunker #7. Yes, during times of impending doom, we would all like a bit of "luck" on our side. As Chaplain Carver would no doubt remind us, however, it was not luck but the living God who protected him and others on that fateful day.

In a similar vein, Retired Army Major Robert Nuttall also re-counts his first incoming in Kuwait, in Operation Desert Storm. He says it was the very moment when he truly gave his life to God. For him, the vulnerability, the inability to control the flight of incoming SCUD missiles, and his keen sense of personal mortality were the factors that led him to the throne of God's sufficiency and grace. This same grace has sustained Robert and his wife, Amy through the challenges of subsequent Posttraumatic Stress Disorder (PTSD), Traumatic Brain Injury (TBI), and related complications. The maxim, "There are no atheists in foxholes" was certainly true for Doug Carver and Robert Nuttall, just as it is for the rest of us.

We are all at war, whether on the battlefront or the home front, whether in the board room or the class room. War is a reality for each of us. We all take incoming.

We all take incoming.

A signature verse from the Bible occurs as Jesus prepares his disciples for the harsh reality, the warfare, they would soon face (underline added): "In the world you <u>will</u> have tribulation..." (John 16:33, NKJV). This passage, along with a multitude of other biblical references to the same concept, highlights the certainty that tribulation will come our way. Additionally, the Greek (*thlipsis*) and Latin (*tribulum*) roots of the word *tribulation* lend further insight. John MacArthur, a renowned Bible scholar and commentator, summarizes the following on page 281 of *The MacArthur New Testament Commentary*: Romans 1-8.

> "*Thlipsis* (tribulations) has the underlying meaning of being under pressure and was used of <u>squeezing olives in a press in order to extract the oil and of</u> <u>squeezing grapes to extract the juice</u>...In Scripture the word *thlipsis* is perhaps most often used of outward difficulties, but it is also used of <u>emotional stress</u>."

Building on this definition, Bruce Hurt comments on his P-R- E-C-E-P-T A-U-S-T-I-N website (http://www.preceptaustin.org/ romans_53-5.htm):

> "The English word "*tribulation*" is derived from the Latin word *tribulum* (literally a thing with teeth that tears), which was a heavy piece of timber with spikes in it, <u>used for threshing the corn or grain.</u> The *tribulum* was drawn

over the grain and it <u>separated the wheat from the chaff</u>.
As believers experience the "tribulum" of tribulations,
and depend on God's grace, the trials purify us and rid
us of the chaff."

These word origins help us understand and identify with
tribulation to a far greater degree. We will all be squeezed and
what is inside of us will come out—for each of us the leakage will
be either resignation or resilience. We will all be threshed, and the
wheat of our lives will be separated from the chaff, ideally
allowing us to be purified and refined in the process.

> For each of us the leakage will be either
> resignation or resilience.

Predicting Simon Peter's denial of His Lord amidst the duress
of public questioning, Jesus warns Peter in Luke 22:31,32
(underlines added): "Simon, Simon, behold, Satan has demanded
permission to <u>sift you like wheat</u>; but I have prayed for you, that
your faith may not fail; <u>and you, when once you have turned again,
strengthen your brothers</u>."

Jesus is telling Peter he will deny his very core values and his
love for Jesus, yet "once you have turned again" (bounced back)
you will "strengthen your brothers (help others)." Although victory,
joy, and ministry to others are achievable through the power of
Christ; the Biblical narrative and our own life stories reflect that
we all experience "sifting" amidst the reality of tragedy, trial, and
tribulation.

Yes, <u>we all face the reality and nature of tribulation</u>. No doubt you, like me, are anxious to discuss "the good stuff" — bouncing back, overcoming against all odds, resilience. But first we have to do the hard work of understanding tribulation and the resulting trauma we are up against. Working with trauma sufferers, including many with the mental, emotional, and spiritual wounds of war, I know how critical it is for the sufferer to recognize that evil (and sin in a Biblical sense) exists in this world. Pain and suffering are consequences of this evil, and none of us are immune to them.

The warrior who does not intellectually or emotionally recognize the existence of evil and the reality of pain and suffering is more subject to being blindsided, swept totally off of their feet. One would hope that the church would prepare people for the reality of suffering in the world about them. Generally speaking, this needs to improve. Having discussed military trauma with hundreds of pastors and church leaders over the past several years I have been dismayed to see a widespread prosperity gospel mentality developing. Such an approach maintains that if you believe and work hard enough, trust God hard enough, and pray hard enough, you can have everything you want: security, money, peace, and well- being. This prosperity gospel approach denies the reality and the theology of suffering, not giving proper emphasis that "He causes His sun to rise on the evil and the good, and sends rain on the righteous and the unrighteous." (Jesus' words from Matthew 5:45) A prosperity gospel marginalizes many Godly examples of faithful men and women over the course of history for which God's answer to fervent prayer was packaged in delay and a clouded future of continued suffering.

Many a pastor who has become more acutely aware of the trauma of our nation's wounded warriors and families, has commented to me that he needed to go back to seminary to understand and guide others in the Theology of Suffering. Ironically, the theology of suffering is often best seen in the crucibles of military training. Recognizing this need to prepare our troops to confront the harsh reality of evil on the battlefield, our nation's training centers for new military recruits, boot camps, have increased the training time spent on moral, emotional, and spiritual factors. It is far better to have some of these foundational principles nailed down *before* the storm hits, *before* your best buddy is killed, *before* you have to take a life, *before* lifelong injuries are sustained in the course of military duties, or *before* the trials and tribulations in every walk of life occur.

Following the wisdom of ancient Chinese warrior Sun Tzu, "If you know your enemy and know yourself, you need not fear the result of a hundred battles." But Sun Tzu warned, "If you know yourself but not the enemy, for every victory gained you will also suffer a defeat." Hence, let us better understand the enemies of our souls: the evil of our world, the evil in our own lives, and the supernatural evil of which the Bible warns us: "Be of sober spirit, be on the alert. Your adversary, the devil, prowls around like a roaring lion, seeking someone to devour." (I Peter 5:8)

Evil Is Real

The <u>evil of our world</u> is pervasive. In the fall of 2002 my wife, Kathleen, and I visited Vilnius, Lithuania. We toured the now extinct Soviet KGB Prison. It had been converted into a KGB Museum, or as it was more commonly known in Lithuania, "The Museum of Genocide Victims." The fifty year occupation of Lithuania by the Soviet Union was brutal, particularly for those who were sent to Siberia under the harshest of conditions and maltreatment. The history of Lithuania under Communist domination is an amazing story of individual and collective resilience, but the harsh reality is that evil was present and took its toll.

We were privileged to be escorted around the prison by Catholic Archbishop Sigitas of the Archdiocese of Kaunas. Father Sigitas is called by many, "The Face of Lithuania" for his resistance to the Communist state. At the risk of death Father Sigitas remained faithful. He taught young children about God. He published an underground newspaper to encourage the Lithuanian people. He never bent his knee in submission to communism. He simply would not deny his faith. He would not bow to the false god of atheism that his captors offered him and other faithful people of his country. He was a true profile in courage. He was a model of resilience. He did not waver. And he suffered mightily for his stance.

Father Sigitas first showed us the room where he had been held in the KGB Prison in Vilnius for six months, before he was deported to Siberia for his ten year sentence at hard labor, mercifully curtailed at four and a half years by the fall of the Berlin Wall and the liberation of Lithuania in 1990. He then showed us rooms where he had been tortured in despicable ways. We paused in a room with a small stone footstool in the middle, hearing him tell of standing on the stool while his captors filled the room with freezing water from the nearby river. Standing with sub-zero water up to the neck soon became unbearable, causing the prisoner to cry out in delirium as he was questioned endlessly. We also noted the solitary confinement room where prisoners were kept in total darkness, just as the State sought to keep the freedom loving Lithuanian people in the total darkness of domination.

He then ushered us into the basement. This was an experience for which we were ill prepared. We entered The Execution Chamber. Noting the bullet holes still in the walls, we could see where the KGB guards had carved out a corner of this room so the blood of the slain would drain more readily.

At this moment Kathleen, with tears in her eyes, turned to me and said, "Ronald Reagan was right. There really are evil empires." Yes, my dear bride had summarized it well. <u>Evil empires do exist with evil leaders who perpetuate trauma, tragedy, and tribulation</u>. The Soviet Union under Stalin (the Siberian Gulags), Nazi Germany under Hitler (extermination of 6 million Jews in the Holocaust), Cambodia under Pol Pot (the "Killing Fields"), Liberia under Charles Taylor ("child soldiers"), and Iraq under Saddam Hussein ("gassing of the Kurds") are prime examples among others too numerous to enumerate. Evil empires and evil people exist and they bring pain, suffering, and tribulation into our world. The world will never be free of them.

> Evil empires do exist with evil leaders who perpetuate trauma, tragedy, and tribulation.

As well, we must recognize <u>our own evil nature</u>. Since the fall of Adam mankind has been beset with a sinful nature which often results in painful consequences for us and others. In the Bible the Apostle John puts this in context (italics added): "For everything in the world—*the cravings of sinful man*, the lust of his eyes and the boasting of what he has and does—comes not from the Father but from the world." (I John 2:16, NIV) Connecting these sinful cravings to the war that rages in and around us personally, the Apostle Peter states, "Dear friends, I urge you, as aliens and strangers in the world, *to abstain from sinful desires, which war against your soul.*" (I Peter 2:11, NIV)

Peter continues later to highlight the <u>active role of a supernatural Satan</u> who also wages war against the human race, "Be self-controlled and alert. Your enemy the devil prowls around like a roaring lion looking for someone to devour." (I Peter 5:8, NIV)

Evil is a reality in our world, it also comes packaged in our own sinfulness, and it supernaturally appears in the form of fallen angelic beings who wage war against our souls. Evil results in tribulation. This is real for each of us, and it hurts.

Tribulation Is Real

In the simple terms of the *Merriam-Webster's Student Dictionary*, Tribulation: n.; "1 : distress or suffering resulting from cruel or unjust treatment or misfortune 2 : a trying experience." (Used by permission. From *Merriam-Webster's Student Dictionary* ©2007 by Merriam-Webster, Incorporated, www.WorldCentral. com.)

Tribulation is often defined more personally, however. Perhaps it's the loss of <u>your</u> house, <u>your</u> job, or <u>your</u> closest loved one. Perhaps it's the privation of <u>your</u> health, or <u>your</u> life's work, or <u>your</u> reputation. Perhaps it's a crisis of faith, or a "dark night of the soul." Perhaps it's the total devastation of natural disasters: earthquakes, tsunamis, hurricanes, tornadoes, flooding, or fires. The list is endless.

In *Night Shift* (page 45), author Dave Shive notes a broad range of possible tribulation scenarios which perhaps you can identify with.

- Trapped in a stale or lonely marriage
- Suffocated by a dead end career
- Despairing over rebellious children
- Burdened by deteriorating health
- Surviving the death of a loved one
- Strapped by mounting bills with little income
- Defeated by educational failure
- Humiliated by criticism and rejection

- Discouraged by childlessness
- Betrayed by a friend
- Oppressed by the dark gloom of clinical depression
- Frustrated by lack of a ministry appearing to go nowhere
- Arriving at old age and feeling useless
- Addicted and helpless to overcome the addiction
- Single but yearning for a spouse

We add more tribulation scenarios which are commonly experienced by troops, veterans, and military families today:

- The grind of repeated deployments which often leave fatigue and discouragement in their wake
- The reality of Combat Trauma, Posttraumatic Stress Syndrome, and related issues
- The reality of Secondary Trauma in spouses and families
- The impact of physical, mental, emotional, relational, and spiritual wounds which are slow to heal, if ever

God Is Real

Most of us in the real world do not question the reality of evil, sin, suffering, and tribulation. Many, however, do question the existence of God or His good character. Common reasoning goes like this: "God, if You are good and loving, if You created this earth, then why is there so much pain? Why is there suffering in this world? And, in particular, God, why does it have to come down on me? I am a good person. What have I done wrong? I don't deserve this!"

In *The Upside of Down*, Joe Stowell states: "The trouble with trouble is that it threatens not just our comfort and peace but our faith in God." (pg 43) Many resources (see Additional Study at end of chapter) provide deeper study and analysis of the basic questions which accompany tribulation and trauma. If these questions go unaddressed, they often result in a crisis of faith when tough times occur.

Perhaps one of the greatest written examples is the story of Job, recorded in the book of Job, the oldest book in the Bible. Job was a man of God who got body slammed in every sense of the word, yet remained faithful, trusting His Creator no matter what. Despite discouraging "friends" and a wife who eventually told him to "Curse God and die" (Job 2:9). Job worked his way through the debilitating trauma and eventually proclaimed "Though He slay me, I will hope in Him." (Job 13:15)

From the life of Job and so many other resilient figures, as well as my own life experiences, I conclude the following: While it is important to understand the reality and nature of evil and suffering in our world, it is far more important to understand the true character of God which trumps these realities.

When troops in harm's way hold hands and pray before a dangerous mission, they are not discussing esoteric philosophies or the origin of suffering. They are crying out to the living God: "O

Lord, you are our Rock, our Fortress, our Deliverer, our God in Whom we take refuge... our shield and the horn of our salvation, our strong- hold... In our distress we call upon You, Lord... we cry to You for help." (Psalm 18:1, 2, 6, paraphrase)

When incoming happens to you and to me, it is far more important to cling to the living God with the sure knowledge that God still loves us, God remains all-powerful, God suffers with us and feels our pain, God refines us through the suffering, God can turn evil into good, and God comforts us so that we can comfort others.

Jesus' words are real and relevant (emphasis added): "These things I have spoken to you, that in Me you <u>may have peace</u>. In the world you <u>will</u> have <u>tribulation</u>;"

His words are also comforting, leaving us with hope: "but be of good cheer, I have overcome the world." (John 16:33, NKJV)

> While it is important to understand the reality and nature of evil and suffering in our world, it is far more important to understand the true character of God which trumps these realities.

ADDITIONAL STUDY:

1. Kushner, Harold. *When Bad Things Happen to Good People*. New York: Anchor Books, 2004.
2. Lewis, C. S. *The Problem of Pain*. New York: Harper Collins, 2001. First published 1944 by Macmillan.
3. Schaeffer, Edith. *Affliction: A Compassionate Look at the Reality of Pain and Suffering*. Grand Rapids: Baker Books, 1993

2

Humpty Dumpty Had a Great Fall
Understanding the Nature of Trauma

Humpty Dumpty sat on a wall,
Humpty Dumpty had a great fall.
All the King's horses, And all the King's men
Couldn't put Humpty together again!

Most of us have heard of Humpty Dumpty, the nursery rhyme character who had a great fall, who experienced great trauma. For me, the image is of an egg on top of a wall which falls and splats, never to be put together again. Perhaps you have a different image (maybe even from your own life experience), but the end result is the same: catastrophic failure, severe trauma, destruction.

Regrettably, this picture defines trauma: an earth-shattering, gut-wrenching, inexplicable experience that leaves us in pain, in doubt, in crisis. While we will work to avoid the smashed egg experience through resilience, the reality is that trauma is real, it hurts badly, and it does not simply diminish or quickly go away.

Trauma on the Edge of Evil

"What should I tell him? Jacob just called from Afghanistan... Something horrible has happened." Georgia National Guard Infantryman Jacob Callaway's unit was on an operation in a small village. He was assigned point as his fire team entered a house, having exchanged fire with Taliban insurgents who had taken cover there. In what is always a tremendous act of courage, bravery which overcomes the wrenching fear of entering an unknown room with an unknown and deadly enemy, Jacob is first through the door. Face to face with an insurgent, it is kill or be killed. As Jacob returns fire, the insurgent grabs a young girl to use as a human shield. Jacob kills the young girl and the insurgent. In the blink of an eye, he experiences something that will haunt him for a lifetime. He did not intend this; it runs counter to everything he stands for, it makes him want to vomit, it generates false guilt for something out of his control, it causes him to question the nobility of his cause, it makes him want to quit.

"What should I tell him?" Jacob's mom, Dr. LuAnn Callaway, a professional counselor herself, asks again. My response is this: "Tell him that he has been standing on the edge of evil. He has just looked evil square in the face. This is what evil does—it takes away hope, basic human rights and liberties, and ultimately breath and life itself from the innocent. Were it not for you, Jacob, and so many other men and women who stand guard on freedom's frontier around the globe, this world would truly be depraved. I know this is very hard. Thank you for standing in the gap on our behalf. Don't question your calling as a soldier. Your cause is noble and right and just. This is not your fault. Thank you for serving, Jacob. I love you. God loves you. We will get through this together."

"In the world you will have tribulation..." and the result of tribulation is trauma such as this, a reality for so many of our troops at the point of the spear. It's the reality for the moms and dads, wives and husbands, family and friends who love the selfless servants who go into harm's way on our behalf.

An oft-quoted British Statesman and Philosopher in the 1700s, Edmund Burke, said, "All that is necessary for the forces of evil to win in the world is for enough good men to do nothing." Where would we be without the good men and women who "do something" in the face of evil? Gratefully, we don't have to ask that question. They are there in our military, police and fire services, our families and communities, and our nation. Yet, when good men and women such as Jacob, stand as noble warriors, resisting evil in this world, they are frequently wounded, traumatized physically, mentally, emotionally, relationally, and spiritually.

So it is with each of us. As warriors, we also get wounded. Some of the wounds we can see. Some are hidden. Some heal in a short time. Others take a lifetime.

> When good men and women such as Jacob, stand as noble warriors, resisting evil in this world, they are frequently wounded, traumatized physically, mentally, emotionally, relationally, and spiritually.

Further Defining Trauma

The wounds of trauma that are often the most challenging come from the spiritual dimension, the wounds of the heart, soul, and spirit which must heal from the inside out.

Trauma is the Greek word meaning "wound." The word also means "damage or defeat." The New York University Child Study Center provides a useful and comprehensive definition of trauma:

> "A traumatic situation is one involving an actual or threatened death or serious injury. Sometimes when people experience an event so terrible and frightening that it is difficult for most of us to imagine, they suffer from shock. This can happen after a one-time natural catastrophe like a hurricane or a flood or after an experience like seeing a bomb attack or seeing someone shot. Sometimes this kind of shock can happen when an unpleasant experience occurs time and time again in a child's life (or an adult), like being beaten or sexually abused repeatedly.

> "Particular signs of stress can occur after experiencing an event directly, from witnessing an event, or even hearing about such an event in regard to a family member. People who suffer from a prolonged reaction to such shock may be

diagnosed as having Post Traumatic Stress Disorder."

Writing for The National Center for Post-Traumatic Stress Disorder (PTSD), Dr. Merle R. Jordan augments the description above with *A Spiritual Perspective on Trauma and Treatment*. While this entire article is worth reading, and applicable far beyond a military setting, the following extract makes the cogent point regarding spirituality and trauma (underlined by author for emphasis): "Whether a clinician is an avowed religious person or not, a clinical perspective cannot overlook <u>agonizing spiritual questions</u>... Beyond the unfathomable question of why it happened, the survivor confronts another equally incomprehensible question, '<u>Why me</u>?' The arbitrary, random quality of his or her fate defies the basic human faith in a just or predictable world order. <u>Trauma tears</u> <u>at the very fabric of one's faith.</u> To develop a full understanding of the trauma story, the survivor must examine the moral questions of guilt and responsibility and <u>reconstruct a system of belief</u> that makes sense of the undeserved suffering." (http://www.ncptsd.va.gov/publications/cq/v5/n1/jordan.html)

Some body slams are worse than others, some life traumas resolve quicker than others. We also know that minor traumas left untreated can also grow into long-standing life issues. It is important to identify trauma early, ideally on the milder end of the spectrum before it proceeds to more extreme and persistent conditions. Early identification is critical to balanced and preemptive treatment.

> Early identification is critical
> to balanced and preemptive treatment.

Applying this to a military setting, the traumas resulting from military deployment and combat experiences also range across a spectrum which goes from normal reintegration issues (which resolve quickly) to combat operational stress issues (which lend themselves to early intervention by lay and professional counselors) to the most severe condition of PTSD, a Diagnostic and Statistical Manual (DSM) IV diagnosable, persistent, and serious medical condition which needs definitive longer term care. Although many lesser complications are termed "PTSD" by lay persons and the media, casually referencing all mental health issues as PTSD is not useful, potentially causing an undue focus on the darker side when time and healthy reintegration into the normality of life will often suffice. The same comment regarding a <u>spectrum</u> of severity holds true for secondary trauma in the lives of those who love and care for trauma sufferers.

We must conclude that trauma is real. It is serious. It impacts the total person, mind, body, and soul. Trauma is no respecter of persons, it occurs across a broad spectrum of conditions, life experiences, and severity. We also must conclude that recovery from trauma takes time and significant effort.

Avoiding the Misconceptions of Trauma

In *The Upside of Down*, Joe Stowell gives us a head start on resilient thinking when he states, "Responding well to trauma demands that we dismiss wrong conclusions about our problems and look to see what is true about the role God plays in the process." Equating pain to trauma, he provides useful categories regarding how we as humans draw the wrong conclusions from our trauma.

Each merits further study, but I have provided a brief expansion on his categories.

- *Pain is punishment*. A vignette in the Gospel of John addresses this well. Jesus' disciples demonstrated confusion about the relationship between the spiritual failure (sin) and suffering when they asked, "Rabbi, who sinned, this man or his parents, that he was born blind?" Jesus answered, "Neither this man or his parents sinned, but that the works of God should be revealed in him." (John 9:1-5, NKJV) Many a well-meaning person has further wounded a trauma sufferer by implying that sin or wrongdoing were the reason for someone's inexplicable tragedy. Although there are times when God brings discipline into our lives and wrongdoing carries consequences which are painful, pain, tragedy, trauma, and tribulation are not punishments from God.
- *Pain is unproductive*. In the vernacular of U.S. Army Rangers, "Pain is weakness leaving the body." The notion is that pain is productive for growth and restoration is a well-accepted principle, but it's easy to forget this when you have just been wounded. Since my early days as a cadet at West Point, I found a Biblical reminder in James very useful in

keeping pain in perspective (underlined for emphasis): "Consider it all joy, my brethren, when you encounter <u>various trials</u>, knowing that the testing of your faith <u>produces endurance</u>. And let endurance have its perfect result, so <u>that you may be perfect and complete, lacking in nothing</u>." (James 1:2-4)

- *Pain indicates spiritual failure.* There are too many counterexamples in the scriptures and the world of those righteous, noble, <u>humble servants of God who get body slammed just like everybody else</u>. Although soul searching during adversity can be useful, particularly when the trauma seems to be the clear consequences of our own actions, the unproductive thought, "I must have done something wrong to deserve this..." leads to <u>false guilt and unproductive angst.</u>

- *Pain is not good.* Romans 8:28, 35, 37 powerfully states, "And we know that God causes <u>all things</u> to work together for good to those who love God, to those who are called according to His purpose... <u>Who will separate us</u> from the love of Christ? Will <u>tribulation</u>, or distress, or persecution, or famine, or nakedness, or peril, or sword? ... But <u>in all these things we overwhelmingly conquer</u> through Him who loved us." These are powerful truths to cling to when the bottom seems to have fallen out. Nothing, including war's worst wounds, can separate us from God's love, and He can transform such pain into good.

- *Pain is incompatible with a God who is good and all-powerful.* Harold Kushner's *When Bad Things Happen to Good People*, pages 6 and 7, states it well: "The misfortunes of good people are not only a problem to the people who suffer and to their families, they are <u>a problem for everyone who wants to believe in a just and fair and livable world</u>. They inevitably raise questions about the goodness, the kindness, even the existence of God." (underlined for emphasis) Our investigation of resilience will illustrate how God's goodness, omnipresence, and omnipotence provide courage and confidence as we struggle with pain in our lives.

Regaining Altitude

Let's gain altitude. With height comes perspective. It is now clear. <u>In the world we have tribulation</u>. You and I simply need to listen to today's news, or remember the body slams of dear family and friends, or think about Job's suffering, or Jacob in Afghanistan, or reflect on our own life experiences and we are convinced.

Trauma results from such tribulation. When trauma is misinterpreted it leads to wrong responses and false conclusions about the role of pain and suffering in our lives, as well as the role God plays through our pain and suffering. Trauma is real and we really need to understand it in order to be resilient through it.

Humpty Dumpty did sit on a wall, and he did have a great fall. How do we mend the broken pieces, how do we properly respond to trauma, how do we bounce back, or even better, how do we bounce to higher levels of personal and professional fulfillment than ever before? As members of the human race, we all periodically cry out, "Mend this broken heart, there's been a great fall—and all the shattered pieces need you most of all." ("Broken Heart" from the album "Do Not Fear" © Bonnie Knopf-Nuggets of Truth BMI)

BOUNCE BUILDERS:

Each remaining chapter of *Resilience God Style* will contain a "Bounce Builders" section, including selections from my audio player "Resilience Playlist," a collection of uplifting and inspirational songs and sermons related to stress reduction, response to trauma, and overall personal resilience. I strongly recommend that you establish your own resilience playlist which captures the songs and other content that uniquely nurture your soul. The companion *Resilience God Style Study Guide* has a section to capture key songs and content for your own resilience playlist.

1. Evans, Darrell. "Trading My Sorrow," as contained in *Freedom.* Nashville: Integrity/Columbia, 1998,
    Note: This song is a wonderful representation of biblical truth regarding resilience and the reality of how God turns mourning and sorrow into joy. It is #1 on my Resilience Playlist.
2. Knopf, Bonnie. "Mend This Broken Heart," as contained in *Close To His Heart*. Portland, OR: Free Rain Records, 1994.
3. Judah Generation. "We Need A Healing," as recorded on *Inspired by…The Biblical Experience.* Grand Rapids: Zondervan, 2006.

ADDITIONAL STUDY:

1. Adsit, Christ. *The Combat Trauma Healing Manual: Christ-centered Solutions for Combat Trauma.* Newport News, VA: Military Ministry, 2007.
2. Cantrell, Bridget C. and Chuck Dean. *Down Range to Iraq and Back.* Seattle: WordSmith, 2005.
3. Hill, Margaret, Harriet Hill, Richard Bagge and Pat Miersma. *Healing the Wounds of Trauma: How the Church Can Help.* Nairobi, Kenya: Paulines Publications Africa, 2004.
4. Tribus, Paul. *The Scars of War.* Seattle: WordSmith, 2005.
5. Vanauken, Sheldon. *A Severe Mercy.* New York: Bantam Books, 1977.

3

Bitter or Better?

Bitter or better? That is the question. Because tribulation is real and trauma is inevitable, we must consider our reactions. "How will we respond to the curve balls of life?" is a real question. "Do we get bitter or better?"

"Okay, Dees. You'll need to sit this one out."

"But Coach... I'm the Captain of the Team!"

The reality was that the other guy had shown himself to be much faster, tougher, and better than I was. The football coach rightfully put "the other guy" in the starting linebacker position. Yet I was the Team Captain, how could this be? At the ripe old age of fifteen I had a very difficult time dealing with such a demotion. My pride and unwillingness to grasp the reality of my waning football career caused me to blame the coach, who became the object of my resentment and the focus of my bitterness.

This bitterness bordered on phobia, lasting for several years, causing me to literally shut down and often dysfunction. On one occasion, the football coach came to watch one of the basketball games in which I was playing. Upon the simple appearance of this coach, my anger, resentment, and bitterness boiled over. I had to leave the game. For me, this became a life lesson, a teachable moment, where I personally realized how destructive bitterness can become in a person's life, and in this case, in my life.

Although it took a few years and spiritual mentoring by others, I was eventually able to maturely look back on the experience. In retrospect, this life lesson was priceless. At an early age God seared the futility of bitterness into my psyche. Little did I know how valuable this lesson would be on the other playing fields and battlefields of life. Above the Field House door at West Point, General Douglas MacArthur's voice puts the pain and sacrifice of athletic strife in perspective for the cadets: "On these fields of friendly strife are sown the seeds that on other days and other fields will bear the fruits of victory." How true this is!

Many of us can relate similar stories of learning valuable lessons like this. Isn't this the way it normally happens? Regardless of age, something doesn't go our way and we think we have to find a scapegoat, a reason, an excuse. Nothing limits this dynamic to the young. Many an adult carries their story of "woulda,' coulda,' shoulda'" to their grave, dying as bitter and angry people. Yet, there is an alternative. Instead of growing bitter, we can grow better.

A more poignant and positive story is that of Gary Beikirch, Vietnam Medal of Honor recipient, and his faithful wife, Lolly. Refer to "Stress and Trauma Care with Military Applications" (American Association of Christian Counselors 30-hour video series) available at http://www.aacc.net for a fuller depiction of the inspiring lives of these wonderfully resilient people.

Gary was a Special Forces (SF) medic with a 5th SF Group detachment in Vietnam, attached to a South Vietnamese outfit in Kontum Province, Republic of Vietnam, 1 April 1970. On that fateful day, the base camp was attacked by thousands of North Vietnamese regulars. When Gary was wounded and immobilized early in the battle, Gary's Montagnard (meaning "mountain people") battle buddy, "Deo," continued to carry Gary about the battlefield to allow Gary to administer urgent medical triage to other wounded warriors.

At one point, a rocket from a distant hill whooshed toward Gary and Deo. Deo blanketed Gary with his body, taking the blast, sacrificing his own life, saving Gary. The battle eventually subsided, with the U.S.-assisted South Vietnamese consolidating their position, allowing for evacuation of the wounded, including Gary, and reconstitution of their defensive position.

Gary's Medal of Honor Citation reflects the following:

> "For conspicuous gallantry and intrepidity in action at the risk of his life above and beyond the call of duty. Sgt. Beikirch, medical aidman, Detachment B-24, Company B, distinguished himself during the defense of Camp Dak Seang. The

allied defenders suffered a number of casualties as a result of an intense, devastating attack launched by the enemy from well-concealed positions surrounding the camp. Sgt. Beikirch, with complete disregard for his personal safety, moved unhesitatingly through the withering enemy fire to his fallen comrades, applied first aid to their wounds and assisted them to the medical aid station.

"When informed that a seriously injured American officer was lying in an exposed position, Sgt. Beikirch ran immediately through the hail of fire. Although he was wounded seriously by fragments from an exploding enemy mortar shell, Sgt. Beikirch carried the officer to a medical aid station. Ignoring his own serious injuries, Sgt. Beikirch left the relative safety of the medical bunker to search for and evacuate other men who had been injured.

"He was again wounded as he dragged a critically injured Vietnamese soldier to the medical bunker while simultaneously applying mouth-to-mouth resuscitation to sustain his life. Sgt. Beikirch again refused treatment and continued his search for other casualties until he collapsed. Only then did he permit himself to be treated. Sgt. Beikirch's complete devotion to the welfare of his comrades, at the risk of his life are in keeping with the highest traditions of the military service and reflect great credit on him, his unit, and the U.S. Army." (http://www.history.army.mil/html/ moh/vietnam-a-l.html)

Little did he know at the time of his combat action and lengthy recuperation from his wounds, but Gary's trauma related to the combat on that fateful day was just the beginning of this life experience. Back in the United States, Gary sought to further his education, attending a college beset with the Vietnam protests of the late sixties and early seventies. Early in his time on campus, some fellow students spat on him and called him a "baby killer," a particularly hurtful epithet for a medic who had risked his life to save young Vietnamese and Montagnard babies. Gary came to the realization that it was "high risk" to remain in this environment, fearful of resorting to violence against such hatefulness toward him. He also recognized that the war had stripped everything out of him. He recognized the need to "refill himself with God."

Faced with these realities, Gary literally went to live in a cave in New Hampshire, also enrolling in a seminary through which he could begin the spiritual refilling process. One day he received a note in his post office box in the nearby town. It read, "Call the Pentagon." Upon calling, he received notification of his Medal of Honor. Another note which he received in that mail box was even more encouraging and fateful. Words of encouragement and love, to the effect, "I have seen you coming into town periodically. I want you to know I am so thankful you made it home alive." These supportive words, penned by Lolly, now Gary's beloved wife of 37 years (and counting!) were the first affirmation he had received from a not-so-grateful nation.

Lolly provides a unique window into the life of a young military bride caught up in a marriage and a nation at war: "Yes, I knew he went to Vietnam. I was young and did not understand the war, but was thankful that he was alive. Then after the first years of our marriage, the after-effects of the war on our marriage became very real—living in a shack in the woods with no electricity or running water. Yes, I was thankful he was alive, but together at home we struggled through the fog of war in our lives and our family received the long term impacts of war. Thank God we had the Holy Spirit to help us get through it all!"

If anyone had justification for anger, bitterness, revenge, a life full of remorse and resentment, it was Gary and Lolly Beikirch. Yet, through the power of Christ, they truly got better instead of bitter. They grew through the adversity of traumatic combat, the betrayal of a nation, the challenges of PTSD, secondary trauma in the family setting, and in the challenges of Lolly's most recent fight against cancer. Despite the adversity, they made and continue to make Christ-centered choices, to seek growth, purpose, contribution, and resilience. As a result, they have made incalculable contributions to the moral fabric of our nation and to the futures of many young people they continue to selflessly serve.

Posttraumatic Growth (PTG)

The concept of getting better and not bitter lies at the heart of a psychological term called Posttraumatic Growth (PTG). Gary and Lolly Beikirch's life experience ably demonstrates PTG, a subject about which the Psychology Department at the University of North Carolina (UNC) has done extensive research. One of the UNC websites provides useful introductory information (underlined emphasis added) is http://ptgi.uncc.edu/whatisptg.htm.

> "What is posttraumatic growth? It is <u>positive change</u> experienced as a result of the struggle with a major life crisis or a traumatic event. <u>Although we coined the term posttraumatic growth, the idea that human beings can be changed by their encounters with life challenges, sometimes in radically positive ways, is not new</u>. The theme is present in ancient spiritual and religious traditions, literature, and philosophy. What is reasonably new is the systematic study of this phenomenon by psychologists, social workers, counselors, and scholars in other traditions of clinical practice and scientific investigation.

> "What forms does posttraumatic growth take? <u>Posttraumatic growth tends to occur in five general areas</u>. Sometimes people who must face major life crises develop a <u>sense that new opportunities</u> have emerged from the struggle, opening up possibilities

that were not present before. A second area is a change in relationships with others. Some people experience closer relationships with some specific people, and they can also experience an increased sense of connection to others who suffer. A third area of possible change is an increased sense of one's own strength – "if I lived through that, I can face anything". A fourth aspect of posttraumatic growth experienced by some people is a greater appreciation for life in general. The fifth area involves the spiritual or religious domain. Some individuals experience a deepening of their spiritual lives, however, this deepening can also involve a significant change in one's belief system."

Further, UNC provides some valuable clarifications which put PTG in proper context:

"Most of us, when we face very difficult losses or great suffering, will have a variety of highly distressing psychological reactions. Just because individuals experience growth does not mean that they will not suffer. Distress is typical when we face traumatic events.

"We most definitely are not implying that traumatic events are good – they are not. But for many of us, life crises are inevitable and we are not given the choice between suffering and growth on the one hand, and no suffering and no change, on the other.

"Posttraumatic growth is <u>not universal</u>. It is not uncommon, but neither does everybody who faces a traumatic event experience growth.

"<u>Our hope is that you never face a major loss of crisis</u>, but most of us eventually do, and perhaps you may <u>also experience an encounter with posttraumatic growth</u>."

The concept of PTG is a useful launch point as we seek to build bounce, as we pursue resilience. In their 2004 *Posttraumatic Growth: Conceptual Foundations and Empirical Evidence*, Richard G. Tedeschi and Lawrence G. Calhoun from University of North Carolina Charlotte laid the conceptual and statistical foundations for the notion that positive change (posttraumatic growth) can occur from life struggles which they call "seismic events." After a seismic event occurs, they postulate a process which describes the challenges and the response path which can result in positive growth and wisdom for future life struggles.

Although the Tedeschi and Calhoun model explaining how one processes trauma into growth focuses on responses and results <u>after</u> a seismic event, I offer that there is an equally important "upstream" consideration to posttraumatic growth. Specifically, what can one do in a preventive fashion that will "set the conditions," or predispose one to respond in a manner that promotes positive growth. This then leads to a "Before, During, and After" paradigm.

Considering the "During" phase, the seismic event is the body slam, the traumatic occurrence, the life altering experience. Moving past the seismic event, one comes to a fork in the road, the better path or the bitter path, which separates into an upward road of post adversity resilience or a downward road of despair and dysfunction.

The thesis, and the observed reality, is that trauma and adversity can produce growth: spiritual growth, clarified purpose for life, enhanced perception of self, greater contribution to society, enriched relationships, and new ability and opportunity to help others. We have all observed this in our own lives, and in the lives of others. Conversely, the traumatic event can result in a downward spiral which results in undesirable and often tragic outcomes: post- traumatic stress, isolation, anxiety, anger, violence, sexual assault, divorce and other family dysfunction, substance abuse, addictions, posttraumatic stress disorder, and suicide.

At this point, one logically asks: "How do I take the higher, healthier path?" Or, "How do I pull out of the power dive I am in, to get back to the higher path?" For the person who is already in the power dive, recovery may come from residual inner strength, the affirmation and support of family and friends, the intervention of mental health and pastoral professionals, or the powerful impact of peer mentors who "have the T-Shirt" and can engage in mutual trust and confidence.

While near term response to the seismic event, as well as longer term responses to bounce back are critically important; an even more far-sighted issue becomes the <u>preventive steps</u> one takes to enhance their resilience, the "ounce of prevention worth a pound of cure." One's mindset going into trauma heavily influences the way one views trauma, and predisposes them to become either bitter or better. Desirably, one builds resilience ahead of the traumatic event and achieves a mindset, an inclination, to rather view trauma as an opportunity for growth, an obstacle of adversity which is actually a "cleverly disguised opportunity."

"How to I take the higher, healthier path?"

Through the resilient mindset of a Corrie Ten Boom as reflected in her book, *The Hiding Place,* the lice in their concentration camp barracks were actually a "blessing" which discouraged frequent visits by the guards. Viewed through the spiritual lens of 2 Corinthians 4:17, (NLT): "For our present troubles are small and won't last very long. Yet they produce for us a glory that vastly outweighs them and will last forever!"

Posttraumatic Growth in Action: Joseph

So what does PTG look like? Consider a man who was betrayed by his brothers, thrown into a pit to die, sold into slavery in a foreign country, rose to a very prominent position serving a foreign king, was falsely accused and wrongly imprisoned, proved himself a faithful and wise prisoner, was brought full circle to lead the country during traumatic times, and granted sustenance and forgiveness to the very family members that initially betrayed him. If anyone possessed opportunities to grow bitter, to strike back, to get even with his betrayers, his accusers, his captors, he did! Yet, this man was able to grow through adversity into an arena of self-actualization and contribution that he or others would have never anticipated or predicted.

The man described above is in fact Joseph from the Book of Genesis. The final act of his drama ends this way when Joseph replied to his brothers, "But Joseph replied, 'Don't be afraid of me. Am I God, that I can punish you? You intended to harm me, but God intended it all for good. He brought me to this position so I could save the lives of many people. No, don't be afraid. I will continue to take care of you and your children.' So he reassured them by speaking kindly to them." (Genesis 50:19-21, NLT). This story could just as easily been lifted from the headlines of today's paper: betrayal, violence, trauma, a choice between bitter or better, and the outcomes of anger and desperation, or growth and fulfillment. Joseph took the fork in the road towards growth. That's the one I want. This path is well depicted in Dr. Jerry White's *The Joseph Road,* a powerful book which frames the choices we all have before us, choices that determine our destiny, just as Joseph's choices determined his destiny as a person and as the leader of a nation.

Hope or Bitterness

While there are many factors which promote PTG, spiritual elements are unquestionably central to one's ability to choose the harder but more rewarding path of growth. During the time I was commanding the "Fighting Eagles" (1st Battalion, 8th Infantry) at Fort Carson, Colorado, Dr. Jerry White (author of *The Joseph Road* referenced in the previous paragraph), retired Air Force Major General and International President Emeritus of the Navigators, taught our Sunday School class at Pulpit Rock Church in Colorado Springs. During one class he reflected on the tragic murder of his young adult son. In that moment he stated, "As we grow older, if we are growing spiritually, we grow in hope. If we do not continue to grow spiritually, we grow in bitterness."

I have found this to be very true. Whether for an aspiring teenage football player, or a Vietnam Medal of Honor Recipient, or a senior leader in the nation of Egypt in Biblical times, continuing spiritual growth leading to a mature outlook toward adversity proved pivotal.

Whether you are a young wounded warrior whose future has been changed forever, or a businessman whose life's work has been negated by a sudden reversal, or a senior citizen facing mortality in the twilight of your life, this spiritual dynamic is essential. Through spiritual engagement and growth we all can prosper in hope, avoiding the debilitating shackles of bitterness, growing through adversity. This is the "secret sauce" of resilience which will be discussed at greater lengths in forthcoming chapters.

BOUNCE BUILDERS:

1. Byram, Danny. "Broken Pieces," as recorded in *High Places*. Nashville: DBM, Inc., 2008.
2. Knopf, Bonnie. "When I Cry," as recorded in *Do Not Fear*. Portland, OR. Nuggets of Truth, 2009.
3. O'Brien, Michael. "Contentment," as recorded in *Be Still My Soul*. Franklin, TN: Wildwood Studios, 2010.
4. Smiley, Scott. *Hope Unseen: The Story of the U.S. Army's First Blind Active-Duty Officer*. With Doug Crandall. New York: Howard Books, 2010.

ADDITIONAL STUDY:

1. Jordan, Merle R. "A Spiritual Perspective On Trauma and Treatment." *National Center for PTSD Clinical Quarterly* 5, no. 1, (Winter 1995): 9-10.
2. Shepard, Ben. *A War of Nerves: Soldiers and Psychiatrists in the Twentieth Century*. Cambridge: Harvard University Press, 2001.
3. Stanley, Charles. *How to Handle Adversity*. Nashville: Thomas Nelson, 1989.
4. White, Jerry. *The Joseph Road: Choices That Determine Your Destiny*. Colorado Springs: NavPress, 2010.

4

Resilience Life Cycle ©
Bouncing Back, Again and Again

"It was the first day of the term, and 16 West Point cadets were filing into their C Hour class in Leadership in Thayer Hall. At 09:50, the instructor called the class to attention, received the attendance report from the section marcher, and told the cadets to take their seats. 'There's one interesting thing you should know about me,' the instructor said, 'I'm blind. I can't see anything. So, raising your hand in this class is pretty much going to be a waste of time.' The cadets laughed. It was a joke. Everyone knows there are no blind officers in the army." (http://www.blindteachers.net/west-point.html)

Yet there are blind officers in today's Army. Captain Scotty Smiley is one of them. Scotty's amazing story of resilience is best captured in his book, *Hope Unseen*. Scotty and Tiffany Smiley's life experiences compose that priceless "picture worth a thousand words" which allows us to observe resilience in action. I encourage you to read Scotty's inspiring book. We will revisit this amazing couple after I introduce the model which will guide the remainder of our discussion in *Resilience God Style, the Resilience Life Cycle ©*

RESILIENCE LIFE CYCLE©

LEARN & ADAPT

Building Resilience

Weathering the Storm

Bouncing Back

Before **During** **After**

We'll dive into the Resilience Life Cycle© in greater detail in later chapters. For now, note that the Resilience Life Cycle© parallels the posttraumatic growth discussion of Chapter 3: "Before, During, and After" trauma is paralleled by "Before, During, and After" resilience. Note the feedback loop above which implies an iterative nature to this process, refilling the well of courage while restoring and gaining new resiliency in preparation for the next inevitable body slam. With the Smiley's permission and from our personal knowledge of their amazing journey, we briefly map their story of resilience into this Resilience Life Cycle©.

Before

> This is the preventive phase and we all must consider and act upon it.

We are warriors, all of us. As warriors, we must be prepared. We can build bounce and increase resilience ahead of time before encountering the next tribulation and trauma that are sure to come. This is the preventive phase and we all must consider and act upon it.

The best Biblical exhortation for this phase is "Put on <u>the full armor of God</u>, so that you will be able to <u>stand firm</u> against the schemes of the devil." (Ephesians 6:11, underline emphasis added). Scotty Smiley received spiritual nurture from growing up in a Christian home. He learned about the armor of God. During his West Point years this continued and prepared him to arrive on the battlefields of life, and the battlefield of Iraq as a spiritually fit soldier.

Scotty's fitness in other areas, physical, mental, emotional, and relational was equally sound. In U.S. Army terms, he was "comprehensively fit" as a soldier and young leader. In her own way so was Tiffany, his wife. Scotty and Tiffany were part of a healthy relational network of family, friends, and professional comrades. They enjoyed bonds of trust and confidence borne out of vibrant faith and common values. In this network they shared the hardships and enjoyments of life.

A familiar Chinese military maxim says, "We train in peace so we will not bleed in war." Scotty was part of a high performing unit that had trained hard in peace and performed well in combat. They were a solid team with good leadership. They understood their calling and their mission, they knew well the rules of engagement, they were practiced in actions on contact, they respected their leadership, they led their soldiers well, and they would never, ever, leave a fallen comrade behind. Even before the fateful VBIED (vehicle borne improvised explosive device) detonated and blinded him, Scotty and every other person in that unit knew they would be taken care of in every way possible.

This is a key aspect of resilience: the knowledge that you are part of a good team—whether a combat unit, sports team, loving family, a supportive faith and community group—brings confidence and courage as you face potential trauma, and hope and encouragement once the trauma comes.

During

This phase is termed, *Weathering the Storm*.

Among innumerable passages of comfort from the scriptures, a fitting passage is, "God is our refuge and strength, a very present help in trouble. Therefore we will not fear, though the earth should change and though the mountains slip into the heart of the sea;"

(Psalm 46:1, 2). No doubt each military person, business owner, pastor, parent, child, single adult, actually every human being on earth, can identify with the inevitable storms of life, both large and small. None of us are immune. Consistent with the maxim "No Atheists in Foxholes," there are few that turn away God's help in times of severe personal trauma.

From the moment Scotty was wounded a keen awareness of God's help in time of need was critically important to him and the many others who were impacted. While in the early weeks of his rehabilitation Scotty experienced pain, mental anguish, hours of hopelessness, and a sense of extreme and permanent loss, he also overwhelmingly experienced God's love, presence, and comfort. He quickly rebounded from living in bitterness to striving for growth for the betterment of himself and others.

Tiffany went through the same cycle. They would be quick to tell you that their strength, joy, and commitment came from their deep roots of Christian faith. This faith was the predominant factor in their resilient response.

God truly allowed them and others who walked with them, to *weather the storm* with grace and full confidence that God was going through the storm with them. While waves of remorse and doubt understandably roll through periodically, this couple has consistently been remarkably, and some would term miraculously, positive and productive.

After

> This is the transition *from an inward focus,* which is necessary and understandable while working through the initial grief and loss process, *to an outward focus* keyed to contribution and comfort to others.

Having been up close and personal with the trauma of war, the Warrior David said, *"For I am afflicted and needy, and my heart is wounded within me."* Psalm 109:22. This was certainly true of Scotty Smiley. The observable wounds to his eyes and body were evidences certainly, but also the unseen wounds to his heart, soul, and spirit (which often take longer to heal) were acknowledged. With the comfort of his personal faith and the love and support of their rich relational network, Scotty avoided the isolation response often characteristic of such trauma and quickly transitioned *from an inward focus*, which is necessary and understandable while working through the initial grief and loss process, *to an outward focus* keyed to contribution and comfort to others.

Following the iterative nature of the Resilience Life Cycle©, Scotty and Tiffany became predictably stronger and more resilient for the inevitable future challenges of life which would come their way. Overall, together they have become a blessing to many, dispensing hope and light to those languishing in the darkness of despair.

Relating Scotty and Tiffany's experience is not intended to paint the process of before, during, and after as one that is sterile, easy, or automatic. Rather, their story illustrates raw and painful trauma at its worst, the kind of trauma that inconveniently and uncompromisingly intersects one's hopes and dreams for the future.

With the help of God and so many others, Scotty and Tiffany are bouncing "All the Way and Then Some" (a soldier response to the barking of a beloved Drill Sergeant in Boot Camp). Their experience well illustrates the Resilience Life Cycle©.

Tennis Ball or Egg?

I love to play tennis. One of the simple joys is to pop open a fresh can of vacuum packed tennis balls. Whoosh! The smell, the newness, the soft fuzz on the outside cover, and the high and true bounce.

In many ways, this is how we would all like to be: new and BOUNCY! This is a picture of resilience, bouncing back each time after being whacked by a tennis racket wielded by a determined foe, sometimes in the hot sun, sometimes in wet weather, some-times for hour after hour—yet, always bouncing.

Now consider an egg which does not bounce. It splats. Once broken, an egg will never return to its original condition, and certainly never rebound from a fatal fall.

Which are you? Which am I, an egg or a tennis ball? How high do we bounce? Or, do we splat?

"We are pressed on every side by troubles, but we are not crushed. We are perplexed, but not driven to despair. We are hunted down, but never abandoned by God. We get knocked down, but we are not destroyed." (2 Corinthians 4:8, 9, NLT) This is about resilience. All of us should expect to be troubled, in doubt, facing many enemies, and badly hurt at times. Yet, according to the Apostle Paul, *in Christ* we can be resilient, avoiding the egg splat of crushing defeat, desperation, being without friends, and total destruction.

This point is made perfectly clear when the next verse states, "... always carrying about in the body the dying of Jesus, so that the life of Jesus also may be manifested in our body." These words graphically point out our identification with Jesus, our acceptance of Him, and the *personal* victory that comes as a part of that relationship. This life of Jesus in us is the *secret sauce* that fosters spiritual resilience. Combining faith with physical, mental, emotional, and relational factors, we achieve true comprehensive fitness, a fact well illustrated by the Smiley's experience as well as so many others in all walks of life. These are the inspiring faith-filled stories of bouncing back—these can be our stories, too.

During World War II Chief of Staff of the Army, General George C. Marshall declared (underlines added), "I look upon the spiritual life of the soldier as even more important than his equipment... The soldier's heart, the soldier's spirit, the soldier's

soul are everything. Unless the soldier's soul sustains him, he cannot be relied upon and will fail himself and his country in the end... It's morale—I mean spiritual morale—which wins the victory in the ultimate, and that type of morale can only come out of the religious nature of the soldier who knows God and who has the spirit of religious fervor in his soul."
(http://www.quoteland.com/author/General-George-Catlett-Marshall-Quotes/2393/)

Ancient history demonstrated this same theme. The Jewish tradition, later amplified by Jesus, advocated comprehensive fitness long before we did. Mirroring the Shema of Deuteronomy 6:4, Jesus made the case for comprehensive fitness when he responded to the question: "What commandment is the foremost of all?" He responded with the "Great Commandment" recorded for us in Mark 12:29-31 (parenthetical comments added):

> "Jesus answered, 'The foremost is, HEAR O ISRAEL! THE LORD OUR GOD IS ONE LORD; AND YOU SHALL LOVE THE LORD YOUR GOD WITH ALL YOUR HEART (emotional), AND WITH ALL YOUR SOUL (spiritual), AND WITH ALL YOUR MIND (mental), and WITH ALL YOUR STRENGTH (physical). The second is this. YOU SHALL LOVE YOUR NEIGHBOR AS YOURSELF (relational). There is no other commandment greater than these.'"

Let's extrapolate this. The 'heart' is the emotional dimension, the 'soul' the spiritual, the 'mind' the mental, 'strength' physical, and 'loving your neighbor as yourself', relational. God had emotional, spiritual, mental, physical, and relational wholeness figured out a long time ago, in fact, since the beginning of history. Maybe He even knows something about resilience and tennis balls.

In the next three chapters, Before, During, and After we will focus on the Resilience Life Cycle©. We will discover how to become more resilient warriors and help others do the same.

BOUNCE BUILDERS:

1. Alexander, Eric. *The Summit: Faith Beyond Everest's Death Zone.* Green Forest, AR: New Leaf, 2010.
2. Coy, Colonel Jimmie Dean. *A Gathering of Eagles.* 2nd ed. Mobile, AL: Evergreen, 2004.
3. Ten Boom, Corrie. *The Hiding Place.* 35th Anniversary Ed. With Elizabeth and John Sherrill. Grand Rapids, MI: Chosen Books, 2006.
4. O'Brien, Michael. "I'll Rise," as recorded in *Be Still My Soul.* Franklin, TN: Wildwood Studios, 2010.
5. West Point Cadet Glee Club. "Into the Fire," as recorded in *Stand Ye Steady.* West Point, NY: Curtain Call Production, 2005.
6. Billingsley, Charles. "Strength of My Soul," as recorded in *Never Forsaken.* Lynchburg, VA: Charles Billingsley, 2011.

ADDITIONAL STUDY:

1. Sorge, Bob. *Pain Perplexity and Promotion: A Prophetic Interpretation of the Book of Job*. Grandview, MO: Oasis House, 1999.

2. American Bible Society. God Understands Series. 8 Volumes (unnumbered). New York: American Bible Society, 2009.

5

Building Bounce

The Ounce of Prevention

"Taps" always has a haunting sound, but this was my first time. As a "yearling" (sophomore cadet at West Point), I was standing in the West Point Cemetery at the freshly turned graveside of U.S. Army Lieutenant Jonathan "Jon" Shine, West Point Class of 1969. From my foxhole as a plebe the year before, I had known Jon Shine very respectfully as "Sir," given his "first class" (senior cadet) status. I had also known this "man among men" respectfully because of his gigantic faith, his obvious natural gifts ranging from athletics to leadership, and his commitment to Duty, Honor, Country (the hallowed words of the West Point motto) as he served his God, his nation, and his fellow man.

In living, his vibrant walk with Christ made a lasting imprint on all who had the privilege of serving over, with, or under Jon Shine. In dying, he provided a very "teachable moment" for the many gathered at the graveside who anticipated finding themselves on this same path of duty in Vietnam. As well, the Shine family's joyful sorrow was winsome, yet so very hard to understand at that point in my spiritual journey. Gratefully that was about to change.

"Threat clears a man's head." Bob Dees, Barry Willey (I commend Barry's inspiring book about Jon Shine entitled, *Out of the Valley*), Skip Ash, and other future Army lieutenants at graveside that day were very clear headed. Without needing to speak the strong sentiment, we each thought, "That could be me in a short three years." We also asked in our own silence, "Am I ready for this to happen to me, or to others that I love and lead? How high will I bounce when faced with the trauma and realities of war? Do I have the courage, the commitment, the true compassion that it will surely take? What if I become a Prisoner of War (as we heard frequently about the 'Hanoi Hilton,' where incredibly brave captured American service members were imprisoned)? When they strip everything away from me, what will I have left?" The questions rushed through our veins like blood on a vigorous morning of Army PT, but the answers would be slower in arriving. Yes, life would soon come at us very fast, yet God would prove Himself faithful beyond measure.

With a clear head I knew that I was not ready for the uncertain future on my horizon. As a new plebe I had learned about U.S. Army Airborne Jumpmasters, the highly trained leaders in charge of inspecting the individual parachutists rigging before jumps (called JMPI), controlling all actions of parachutists while in flight (including all the Jumpmaster commands, shouted over the roar of aircraft engines, ending with the proverbial "Stand in the Door" and "Go!

Go! Go!"), and last, insuring a safe exit from the aircraft for each jumper in teamwork with the Air Force flight crew.

Later becoming a Jumpmaster myself I was privileged to put my own platoon "out the door" of a C130 Hercules aircraft, experiencing the height of trust and confidence between leader and led, as well as looking into one another's souls as we shared the uncertainty, the esprit de corps and adrenalin of shared risk. Standing at Jon Shine's graveside that cold, dreary November morning, the loudest ringing in my ears was a Jumpmaster giving his first command in the sequence, "Get Ready!" It was almost as if God was the Jumpmaster that day, directing my steps, telling me to get ready spiritually for the challenges and opportunities which most certainly awaited me and those I would lead.

As you perceive by now, we are discussing readiness, the act of being prepared. We are talking about the proverbial "ounce of prevention worth a pound of cure"—the upstream investment of sweat, tears, trying and failing, learning, and practicing to achieve Pavlovian reflexes to do the right thing under the toughest of conditions. In the context of resilience, we are "Building Bounce."

From the last chapter's discussion of the Biblical components of comprehensive fitness (Mark 12:28-31) we know that physical, mental, spiritual, emotional, and relational preparedness are key factors to overall resilience building. We will "water ski" through the more readily understood and accepted arenas of physical and mental fitness, then "scuba dive" into the less researched and recognized discipline of preparing oneself spiritually.

Physical and Mental

Every coach I can remember during my early football days in Texas invoked the familiar saying of Green Bay Packers legend, Vince Lombardi, "Fatigue makes cowards of us all," to highlight the importance of physical fitness as well as its relation to less tangible characteristics such as bravery, cowardice, and bouncing back. Certainly physical fitness is a critical quality and ethic in athletics, in the military and other uniformed professions, and in other marketplaces where fitness conditioning is directly related to task performance. The reality, however, is that physical fitness is important in every endeavor of life, leading to the following benefits:

- Increased strength and ability, to perform tasks with ease and over time
- Enhanced stress reduction, to include release of endorphins and other brain chemicals which promote a sense of emotional wellbeing
- During my first tour in the Pentagon on the Army Staff, one of my fellow "cellmates" (an endearing term used of those who share the long hours and stressful demands of Pentagon life with you) rarely exercised, ate junk food at his desk while working through lunch, smoked whenever possible to calm his nerves, and generally disregarded his own physical preparedness to survive the gauntlet of

never ending Pentagon crises. While a very bright and knowledgeable officer, he soon was under the surgeon's knife for open heart surgery.

- Broader range of recreational opportunities which enhance relational opportunities and provide healthy emotional diversion
- Expanded ability to physical and mentally recover from trauma more quickly

When General David Petraeus was a "Rakkasan" (187th Infantry Regiment) battalion commander in the 101st Airborne Division (Air Assault) at Fort Campbell, KY, he was severely wounded in a training accident, receiving a life-threatening wound from an M16 round through the chest. God preserved his life as he was flown first to the post hospital and then on to a Nashville hospital to be operated on by a surgeon named Bill Frist who later became the Speaker of the U.S. House of Representatives.

Within a week of undergoing thoracic surgery, Dave pulled out an IV tube and got down on the floor to do 50 pushups, in order to demonstrate his readiness to be discharged. And less than three weeks later he was "rucked up" and leading his battalion on an emergency deployment readiness exercise at Fort Bragg, NC.

His superb physical fitness was the key to his physical recovery, combined with years of developing mental toughness and overall resilience. Also demonstrating amazing physical and mental endurance under the load of his most recent commands in Iraq and Afghanistan, I can say with confidence that I'm sure he "did his pushups" this morning before reporting for duty as Director of the Central Intelligence Agency (and he probably ran eight miles, too). (September 2011)

What's the point? Whether you are a busy mom with preschoolers, a stressed businessman constantly tending the bottom line and caring for employees, a missionary nurturing energetic college students, an "11B" (Infantryman) standing on the "edge of evil," the Director of the Central Intelligence Agency, or one who has just experienced "Incoming!" which has turned your world upside down, physical fitness and basic health are critical to your "bounce factor."

The same is equally apparent regarding mental fitness. In recent years the body of knowledge regarding the mental aspects of sports and performance psychology has exploded. Mental preparedness is recognized as critical within the military, professional and college athletics, and other demanding professions.

Related specifically to resilience, mental fitness has both cognitive and affective components. Cognitively, it is important to "know" certain things, such as specific military or professional intelligence, literature and other media, which provide relevant insights and information. Affectively, it is equally important to prepare for healthy psychological responses to adverse circumstances, addressing the resilient mindset to which we have referred before.

After my son, Rob, had experienced his first combat action in Iraq, he responded to me with the often heard exclamation, "The training just kicked in." Mental fitness, mental "toughness," and mental resilience are parts of being prepared. One useful book which further addresses physiological and psychological factors benefiting mental health, resilient response to trauma, and preventative measures is *Your Brain on Joy* by Dr. Earl Henslin.

As a final observation, Posttraumatic Stress Disorder (PTSD) and Traumatic Brain Injury (TBI) have been called the "signature injuries" of our latest conflicts by military leadership, as well as medical and mental health professionals. For example, consider these representative comments from *Science Progress* (parenthetical comment added):

"Across the nation, in hospitals, clinics, and doctor's offices both military and civilian, health care providers are facing unprecedented challenges in dealing with these weapons' results. Among the most puzzling is a set of injuries widely considered a medical 'signature' of this conflict, and one that raises clinical and scientific questions thus far unanswered.

"A major clinical challenge is that the symptoms of the two conditions overlap—although the conditions are very different in their natures—making diagnosis often 'very, very tricky,' Krengel says. (Dr. Maxine Krengel is a clinical neuropsychologist in the Veterans Integrated Services Network of the Department of Veteran Affairs.) TBI causes physiological damage to brain tissue that can result in cognitive deficits and reduced emotional control, among many other problems. PTSD is a learned connection between a traumatic event and a set of responses, which can include nightmares, flashbacks, and constant anxiety and can lead sufferers to alcohol, drugs, and even suicide. But the two conditions share many markers, including sleep disruption, irritability, personality changes, difficulty concentrating and remembering, depression, and more.

"To add to the complication, the presence of one condition can interfere with the treatment of the other." (http://www. scienceprogress.org/2008/12/deciphering-todays-signature-war-injury/)

Hence, traumatic brain injury and post-traumatic stress disorder often form a challenging duo in the minds and hearts of our nation's warriors. While TBI is a force to the head that damages the brain and impairs its function, with the extent and kind of harm depending on the exact location and scope of the injury; PTSD is a terrifying and often disabling anxiety disorder caused by the experience of violent trauma.

The challenge comes in distinguishing between the psychological symptoms of PTSD and the physiological symptoms of TBI. Hence, even differentiating between Physical and Mental versus Spiritual and Emotional is not nearly as simple as one might think. When one adds the stigma of reporting, and the dynamics of human interactions as a relational factor, the complexity becomes even more apparent.

Spiritual, Emotional, and Relational

For the significant majority in our military and our nation to whom spirituality, and in particular a personal religious faith is important, the use of a faith grid is logical and beneficial. While I'll leave it to others to address how Jewish, Muslim, Hindu, and other faith groups can prove relevant to resilient living, I will address spiritual, emotional, and relational dynamics through a Christian faith grid, sticking to what I draw from personal Christian life experience following Biblical precept. "All Scripture is inspired by God and profitable for teaching, for reproof, for correction, for training in righteousness, so that the man of God may be adequate, equipped for every good work." (2 Timothy 3:16) Or, as our Infantry Sergeant might express, "Hey troops, listen up! This stuff really works! Hooah!"

Let's discuss the "stuff that really works" as we *prepare* to be resilient warriors when the incoming occurs. The "Armor of God" passage from Ephesians 6:13-17 is our overarching passage for building resilience:

> "[13] Therefore, take up the full armor of God, so that you will be able to resist in the evil day, and having done everything, to stand firm. [14] Stand firm therefore, HAVING GIRDED YOUR LOINS WITH TRUTH, and HAVING PUT ON THE BREASTPLACE OF RIGHTEOUSNESS, [15] and having shod YOUR FEET WITH THE PREPARATION OF THE GOSPEL OF

PEACE;[16] in addition to all, taking up the shield of faith with which you will be able to extinguish all the flaming arrows of the evil one.[17] And take the helmet of salvation, and the sword of the Spirit, which is the word of God."

We will expand upon six resilience builders:

- Know Your Calling
- Know Your Enemy
- Know Your Friends
- Know Your Equipment
- Deploy with the Right Mindset
- Develop and Rehearse "Actions on Contact"

Know Your Calling

A familiar expression goes "It is hard to remember your objective was to drain the swamp when you are up to your neck in alligators." This is certainly true. When crisis and trauma occur it is very easy to lose your moorings, to forget your objective, to question your calling. The *Merriam-Webster's Collegiate® Dictionary* provides the following definition for calling: *Calling:* n.; "a strong inner impulse toward a particular course of action especially when accompanied by conviction of divine influence." (Used by permission. From *Merriam-Webster's Collegiate® Dictionary* ©2011 by Merriam-Webster, Incorporated, w w w M erriam -W ebster.com).

Calling often implies a deep sense of conviction to pursue noble goals, certainly the case for most enlistees putting on the nation's uniform, or missionaries enlisting in the Lord's work, or the business owner pursuing excellence on behalf of his employees and his family. Calling is very important, particularly when strong winds begin to blow.

As you recall from the story of Jacob in Afghanistan, a first response to the tragic and unavoidable killing of a young child was to want to be out of the Army, to question the nobility and purpose of his mission, to wonder if he was ever *called* to be a soldier in the first place. Part of my initial advice to Jacob was to, "Remember your calling as a soldier." During the trial of Jesus, Peter certainly questioned his call, denying his Lord three times in the public square. During the trauma of the crucifixion and death of Jesus, he went back to his old lifestyle of fishing, forgetting his calling to be a fisher of men. However, his encounter with the resurrected Jesus on the Sea of Galilee (John 21) challenged Peter back to his senses, and to his divine call.

For me, the divine calling of knowing and serving God through a personal relationship with his Son, Jesus was confirmed repetitively during my formative West Point years, just as was my calling to serve my nation as a military officer. My arrival at West Point in July 1968 signaled a few new realities in my life: no Pontiac, no privileges, and no status as a "plebe" (the lowest life form on campus). I looked at the realities of service and sacrifice ahead of me and concluded that I didn't have "the right stuff." I knew if I dug really deep into my soul, I would come up empty handed.

Through the sponsorship of a math professor and his wife, then Captain Andy (and Gail) Seidel, I learned what it meant to truly give my heart to Jesus, and to live for and in Him. The Seidels likewise mentored my future wife, Kathleen, in Biblical living, preparing her for a future as a marriage partner, mother, Army wife ("the greatest job on earth," or so says the T-shirt), and community leader. For me, the most valuable lessons of the West Point years were not learned in the classroom or on the drill field; rather, they were learned in relationships with faithful Christian mentors and leaders. These people taught and modeled things like the Fruit of the Spirit from Galatians 5:22-23: love, joy, peace, patience, kindness, goodness, faithfulness, gentleness, self-control. They demonstrated the seamless integration of faith, family, and profession into a God-honoring life message, and resilient living in the power of Christ. These were the lessons that would prove invaluable on the battlefields of life, where resilience is not a luxury, but an absolute necessity.

I left West Point equipped with spiritual knowledge, Biblical tools, and life skills which were central to my resilience as a person and a leader in the military, business, and ministry. In the words of 2 Timothy 1:12: "...for I know whom I have believed and I am convinced that He is able to guard what I have entrusted to Him until that day."

This same verse of scripture and many others apparently provided confidence, comfort, and eternal security to Major Daniel Webster Whittle, a Union officer who lost an arm at the Battle of Vicksburg. He was taken prisoner by the Confederates and subsequently penned the following lyrics:

> I know not why God's wondrous grace
> To me He hath made known,
> Nor why, unworthy, Christ in love
> Redeemed me for His own.
> But I know Whom I have believed
> And am persuaded that He is able
> To keep that which I've committed
> Unto Him against that day.

(http://www.wholesomewords.org/biography/bwhittle2.html)
"I Know Whom I Have Believed" by Daniel Webster Whittle

Ultimately, when the thunderbolts of life strike you and me, the deep conviction of our calling in God and our calling to serve our family and fellow man, is an important anchor for the soul, a critical source of resilience. At this point, I must ask: "Do You Know Your Calling: your calling to serve God, your calling to serve man?" These are important questions to ask and resolve now, *before* the chaos of trauma causes you to question your most basic values, and God Himself.

Know Your Enemy

The military leader would never think about entering battle without knowing as much as possible about the enemy. So it is with us.

Who is *your* enemy? Let our common sense Infantry Sergeant cut to the chase again: "Sometimes we shoot ourselves. Sometimes others shoot us. Sometimes we just get blindsided by an eighteen-wheeler. You don't know what hit you. Hooah." How does that translate biblically? Consider the following:

- *We shoot ourselves.* In 1 John 2:16, the Apostle John reminds his "little children," "For all that is in the world, the lust of the flesh, the lust of the eyes, and the boastful pride of life, is not from the Father, but is from the world." You may have heard the expression from the world of Pogo, "We have met the enemy, and He is Us." This is reminiscent of the disciples in the Upper Room with Jesus the night before His Crucifixion asking regarding who would betray Christ, "Is it I, Lord?"

  God's Word shines a bright light on our own fallen nature in Romans 3:23-24 (NLT)(underline emphasis added): "For <u>everyone</u> has sinned; <u>we all fall short</u> of God's glorious standard. Yet God, with <u>undeserved kindness</u>, declares that <u>we are righteous</u>. He did this <u>through Christ Jesus</u> when he <u>freed us from the penalty</u> for our sins."

  In Chapter 2 we discussed some misperceptions regarding pain and trauma, namely that they are solely the result of our own sinfulness. Yet, if you and I are totally honest, we must agree that we are sinners, we often do the wrong things for the wrong reasons, and we rebel against God in a variety of ways. We see it in our own lives and we see it daily in our national headlines. For me, at least, this is an exercise in the obvious. I am frequently "my own worst enemy." Similarly, the Apostle Paul well expressed his human frustration and his divine hope in the transition verses from Romans 7, "wretched man" to Romans 8, "more than conquerors": "Wretched man that I am, who shall set me free from the body of this sin and death? Thanks be to God through Jesus Christ our Lord. So then, on the one hand I myself with my mind am serving the law of God, but on the other, with my flesh the law of sin." (Romans 7:24, 25)

Part of the battle is against an internal enemy, ourselves. It is a lifelong struggle: fleeing wrong things, pursuing right things. (2 Timothy 6:11) The only hope is a loving and sovereign heavenly Father and His Son, Jesus Christ who frees us from the penalty of sin. "He took our bullet!" It is the power of God's Holy Spirit at work in our lives which frees us from the power of sin. "Who will separate us from the love of Christ? Will tribulation, or distress, or persecution, or famine, or nakedness, or peril, or sword? But in all these things we overwhelmingly conquer through Him who loved us." (Romans 8:35-37)

- *Others shoot us.* Given that all humans possess a fallen nature, we periodically shoot at others, and they periodically shoot at us. Some of the wounds are minor and transient, some create such deep seated distrust that they last for a lifetime, without the redemptive power of God, that is.

Some of this incoming is fired from known enemy combatants, in military terms, "those arrayed against us," and others who can be rightly assessed as agents of evil, those who seek to harm and destroy the innocent, the oppressed, and the unfortunate around the world and in our own country.

Perhaps the most difficult wounds, however, are the wounds that come from friends accompanied by not only physical pain but also by the agony of betrayal, false accusation, and lack of grace that cut deep into the heart, soul, and spirit. In military terms this most tragic outcome is called *fratricide*, the intentional or unintentional wounding of one friendly by another. Ranking a close second are those tragedies which come from the carelessness or irresponsibility of others such as drunk drivers. The "avoidability" of such outcomes is a tragedy in itself.

• *The eighteen-wheeler hits us.* We saw in John, Chapter 9 that neither the blind man nor his parents had sinned. There did not appear to be any deep, dark causative factors—he was just born blind.

Frequently, numbers of natural disasters leave individuals and entire nations reeling. Many ask, "Are these punishments or consequences for wrongdoing?" No. Regardless, they are real. They do devastate people's lives. "In the world you have tribulation." (John 16:33) The only question is, "How High Do You Bounce?"

When the tornado, the hurricane, the tsunami, the floods, the overwhelming powers of creation unexpectedly slam into *you* and not the "other guy" how strong is your resilience? Natural disasters and so many other traumas in our lives are inexplicable. These are honest, heart-throb questions: "Why Me, God?" "Do You Even Care, God?" "Why Now?" These are the events in our lives that only a sovereign and loving God can truly understand. Our challenge is to accept, and trust, and grow, and prosper in Him, despite our human inability to "get it."

- *Satan attacks us.* "Finally, be strong in the Lord and in the strength of His might. Put on the full armor of God, so that you will be able to stand firm against the schemes of the devil. For our struggle is not against flesh and blood, but against the rulers, against the powers, against the world forces of this darkness, against the spiritual forces of wickedness in the heavenly places." (Ephesians 6:12)

These Biblical references to the enemy, Satan, are not merely symbolic. The existence of a real, yet unseen spiritual enemy is the primary motivation to put on the spiritual armor of God. From 1 Peter 5:8 "Your adversary, the devil, prowls around like a roaring lion, seeking someone to devour." Just as we cannot ignore the reality of radio waves which we cannot see, we cannot ignore the reality of spiritual warfare motivated by our unseen but very real adversary, the devil.

The admonition to "know your enemy" is certainly relevant on every battlefield of life. Whether we face the enemy of self, others, inexplicable tragedy, or Satan, we must know our enemy.

Know Your Friends

Such was the case when former Army Captain Nate Self, author of *Two Wars,* returned to the home front after selfless and traumatic service as a combat leader in Afghanistan, followed closely by Iraq. Nate's story of surviving the challenges of combat and the challenges of returning to the unseen wars at home highlights the critical importance of "sheltering trees," a family and friend safety net who would not let him go under. In *Two Wars* (page 309), Nate states the following: "I want to die. I want to kill the man who has taken my place. My family sees the brokenness and they've closed in around me, forming a tight perimeter. No one is going to get in. Or out. Julie won't leave me. My parents won't abandon me."

John Donne, a sixteenth century English poet who was well acquainted with grief, suffering, and resilience, penned these famous words:

No Man Is An Island
No man is an island entire of itself; every man
Is a piece of the continent, a part of the main;
If a clod be washed away by the sea, Europe
Is the less, as well as if a promontory were, as
Well as a manor of thy friends or of thine

own were; any man's death diminishes me,
because I am involved in mankind.
And therefore never send to know for whom
The bell tolls; it tolls for thee.

You don't mean this actually applies to tough Rangers, do you? This doesn't apply to independent and successful business executives, does it? Certainly, busy mothers of young children are exempt from the need for such relationships, aren't they? Or Pastors? Or Chaplains? Or distinguished military leaders? Or aging seniors? The answer is: "Yes." The need for deep relationships is universal. "No man is an island." We all need the unconditional love which springs from deep, authentic friendships; we likewise need to be agents of hope for others. That is the way God made us.

Hence, deep personal relationships, be they family or "friends who stick closer than a brother..." (Proverbs 18:24) are tremendously important in the Resilience Life Cycle©. Given this chapter's emphasis on upstream condition setting, we rightly should ask, "Who are our friends? Who are the sheltering trees (referring to "Sheltering Trees" by New Song, see Bounce Builders at end of his chapter) in our lives that know and love us unconditionally, and who will undoubtedly 'be there' when the next body slam knocks on our door?" "Who are the family and friends who will form a tight perimeter around us, who will not let us go down?" "Furthermore, how do we invest in such friendships, both in terms of being a friend and having friends?" Such questions are at the heart of relational fitness.

From a biblical perspective, there are many injunctions emphasizing the power of close, personal relationships, friendships within which we are able to share our highest joys and our deepest sorrows. For example, Proverbs 17:17 states, "A friend loves at all times, And a brother is born for adversity." This passage highlights both the importance of unconditional love of friends (at all times) and the role of family (a brother) who in God's divine order is best suited to provide love, nurture, and support during difficult times. Whether the source of such friendship lies within our earthly families (prayerfully that is the case for each of us), or within a small circle of intimate friends outside the family, the implication is the same: we all need friends, particularly in times of adversity.

And yet, the Bible also provides a caution regarding friends. "A man of *too many* friends *comes* to ruin, but there is a friend who sticks closer than a brother." (Proverbs 18:24) One must be careful to not confuse quantity with quality in the area of friendships. Although there may be benefits to having hundreds of friends on social media, the reality is that we as humans do not have the capacity to invest in large numbers of deep, genuine, authentic friendships that that "stick closer than a brother." The quantity of such friendships each of us can maintain and nurture is not measured in the hundreds; rather, in single or double digits at the most.

Here are a few upstream suggestions regarding Know Your Friends that will enhance your resilience.

- *Pick your friends wisely*. Select life-giving friends who can speak truth, encouragement, and life into you. Select friends who share common values. As a very effective complement to human relationships, don't forget about "man's best friend" (dogs and other supportive pets), a very real source of love and acceptance, particularly when one faces the rejection and betrayal of fellow human beings. Such dog friends are proving to be highly effective in helping wounded warriors engaged in the physical, mental, emotional, and spiritual healing process.

- *Invest in a small number of genuine friendships*. This investment takes time and intentionality. Hebrews 10:24, 25 states, "and let us consider how to stimulate one another to love and good deeds, not forsaking our own assembling together, as is the habit of some, but encouraging *one another*; and all the more as you see the day drawing near." In a similar vein, Acts 2:42 talks about the friendship practices in the early church where "They were continually devoting themselves to the apostles' teaching and to fellowship, to the breaking of bread and to prayer." We see these early friends learning together, fellowshipping together, enjoying meals together, and sharing their deepest needs and aspirations through prayer to God together. In essence, they spend time together and shared their lives with one another. That is what friends do.

- *Identify your "911" battle buddies*. Insure that you know who you will be able to count on when the chips are down. Who do you call first when trauma strikes?

While this is a good idea for anyone, anytime, it is particularly recommended for those who anticipate challenging waters on the horizon, such as an upcoming military deployment, or serious health issues, or a volatile personal relationship. Similar to the practice of designating God Parents for young children, it is a wise practice to know who we can lean on when the fog of trauma moves into our own lives. Often, these people will be the very ones who you did not abandon in their time of need, ones with whom you have forged bonds of trust and confidence through shared hardship and tough life experiences.

In addition to Know Your Calling, and Know Your Enemy, it is critical to Know Your Friends. Each of the profiles of resilience that we highlight in *Resilience God Style* contains such elements of relational health, critical friendship factors that make a huge difference when the storms of life head our way.

Know Your Equipment

Consider this command from a fictitious military leader: "Okay, troops. Now ground all your equipment. We are going into combat, but I don't think you'll need all that stuff. Yes, I'm not kidding...leave your helmets, your weapons, your flak vests... leave it all behind." We would rightly think this leader was "off his rocker," yet personally and collectively we frequently don't use the equipment, the soul armor that God provides to each of us.

The *Armor of God* is critical equipment for the warrior. There are many great expositions regarding Ephesians 6:13-17. An excellent example I highly recommend is Vietnam Veteran, Stu Weber's book, *Spirit Warrior.* See bibliography for publication information. For now, we focus on one piece of the armor, the "sword of the Spirit, which is the Word of God." (Ephesians 6:17)

The day of Jon Shine's funeral I sensed a heavenly exhortation to "Get Ready!" I was validly concerned about the Prisoner of War scenario. With fellow like-minded future warriors, I recognized that if I hid God's Word in my heart, enemy captors would not be able to strip that from me. I have heard that, "Without need there is no learning," equivalent to, "Threat clears a man's head."

I was suddenly very motivated to study the Word of God, to learn it, and to make it my own by investing in scripture memory. This spiritual discipline became a critical element of preparation for warfare: in life and in the military. Little did I know how this small investment up front would impact my life and service, and provide a form of compound interest which continues to pay dividends to this day.

With the wise counsel and encouragement of others, I started memorizing verses of scripture. For this exercise I recommend the Navigator's excellent *Topical Memory System*™ which allowed me to systemically digest and memorize key verses covering a wide array of life issues. I memorized two verses a week, like clockwork, because I knew the clock truly was ticking. Then, over time, I memorized part or all of key chapters of Scripture, such as these:

- Psalm 139: God's omniscience, omnipresence, and omnipotence
- James 1: "Dear friends, is your life full of difficulty and temptation? Then be happy…"
- Romans Chapters 12, 13: selfless service, brotherly love, and the role of government
- 1Corinthians 13: love
- Psalm 91: the soldier's psalm, "hidden under the shelter of God's wings…"
- Romans, Chapters 7 and 8: life struggle, "Wretched man that I am…" vs. "More than conquerors…"
- Hebrews 12: "running the race"
- 2 Corinthians 4: "The Resilience Chapter" (a recent and ongoing memorization project)

One of the early dividends of internalizing God's Word came in U.S. Army Ranger School, the mountain phase, December 1972. We were at the mountain Ranger camp in Dahlonega, Georgia with a class comprised largely of my West Point classmates, newly minted Army second lieutenants in their last phases of training before going to our first operational assignments. As is normally the case, we were wasted by that point, surviving on minimal food rations, some cutting the back out of our boots despite subzero temperatures, to minimize the pressure on overused Achilles' tendons, many with illnesses (I had pneumonia and frostbite), and utter fatigue from lack of sleep and constant demands on the body, mind, and spirit. In other words, we were exactly where the Army wanted us to be, pressed beyond measure, having to dig deeper than ever before, gaining invaluable insights into self and others.

It was a cold Sunday morning with over a foot of newly fallen snow. We were in a classroom setting for a short burst of instruction before taking to the ice covered hills yet once again. In recent days many had parachuted into their training operations or soon would. We all had run until our bodies were screaming and our minds were numb. We all anticipated yet another patrol over the icy hills of northern Georgia later that day, all of us carrying sixty-plus pound rucksacks. In the large classroom the Ranger students constantly played "jab right, jab left" to keep one another awake.

Just as one of my battle buddies had jabbed me in the ribs to stop my head bobbing I heard my name, "Ranger Dees, front and center..." with further explanation that the Ranger chaplain from a nearby town was snowed in and couldn't reach us for a brief worship service scheduled before our departure for yet another round of patrolling. The Ranger cadre, most of them combat veterans who knew the power of faith even though they seldom mentioned it, recognized that I was a man of faith and could perhaps give a sorely needed word of encouragement. For me, it was not some grand or noble task; rather, "the training just kicked in" when I was squeezed and out came scripture.

In what was certainly divinely inspired relevance, I simply recalled from memory and explained Isaiah 40:31:

"Yet those who wait upon the Lord will gain new strength,
(We sure needed it!)
"They will mount up with wings as eagles,
(Sounds like airborne operations!)

"They will run and not get tired,
   ("All the way and then some!")
"They will walk and not become weary."
   (Give me some of that!)

This became a teachable moment. Future rangers and experienced cadre alike were struck by the *relevance of God's Word to the nitty-gritty of life*. Even today, some of those fellow Rangers recount this as the day that "God broke through," allowing them to recognize that faith is not for sissies; faith in the foxhole is for tough Rangers and all others who have to dig deep as they lead others to accomplish tough missions, as they live warriors' lives of fighting, getting wounded, bouncing back, and fighting again.

The 50th Reunion of my West Point class occurs in 2022. One of the great joys for many will be to recount God's faithfulness, provision, and protection. Some will no doubt remind me of that cold day in the mountains of Georgia when God's Word *brought great reward* as highlighted in Psalm 19:7-11, below (italics added for emphasis):

7 The law of the LORD is perfect, *restoring the soul*;
The testimony of the LORD is sure, *making wise the simple*.
8 The precepts of the LORD are right, *rejoicing the heart*;
The commandment of the LORD is pure, *enlightening the eyes*.
9 The fear of the LORD is clean, *enduring forever*;
The judgments of the LORD are true;
they are *righteous altogether*.

[10] They are *more desirable than gold*, yes, than much fine gold,
Sweeter also than honey and the drippings of the honeycomb.
[11] Moreover, by them Your servant is warned;
In keeping them there is *great reward*."

The "helmet of salvation" represents a personal relationship with God through Jesus. He is the "living WORD" according to John 1. Along with this essential piece of gear, the knowledge and ability to apply God's written WORD, the "Sword of the Spirit," is absolutely critical for the warrior in spiritual preparation who seeks to establish a faith foundation that will weather the many storms of life.

While there are many other pieces of equipment we could discuss such as the shield of faith, loins girded with truth, breastplate of righteousness, combat boots of the Gospel, and other spiritual tactics, techniques, and procedures, the centrality and importance of the study, internalization, and application of Biblical precepts is key to those preparing for battle, those preparing to bounce back.

Resilient Leaders, the second book of *The Resilience Trilogy*, expands further upon this, referencing the Book of Nehemiah, lessons which proved pivotal in dealing with several immediate crises taking command of Second Infantry Division on the Demilitarized Zone (DMZ) in Korea. In short, Nehemiah's blueprint for responding to a leadership crisis (rebuilding the walls of Jerusalem) provided me with encouragement and wisdom in rebuilding the physical and spiritual walls of a U.S. Army Division in crisis (one of ten active divisions at the time). God's Word is the most effective leadership manual ever written, pointing the way for resilient warriors, leaders, and organizations.

Deploy with the Right Mindset

Coach Joe Palone was in rare form on that 1969 cold February morning in Arvin Gymnasium at West Point. "Jab! Jab! Jab!"— Plebe boxing at its best. Young Cadet Dees had never boxed before so I was an eager student, particularly given that one of my first sparring bouts would potentially be with classmate Jim Lyon, a tough, prior-service classmate who was a formidable boxer.

Once again, "Threat clears a man's head!" Coach Palone exhorted, "Keep those hands high… get that stance right… *stay balanced*… move in, move out, side to side… Jab! Jab! Jab!" (*Jab* was Coach Palone's favorite word, if you haven't gathered that by now). So what happened with Jim Lyons? He smacked me in the chops, I dropped my left hand, *lost balance* as I leaned into him, and further accentuated the impact of his right hand landing squarely on my jaw. I went from slightly out of balance to totally wobbly, then onto the canvas. Coach Palone was right, "Start with a good stance. Do everything possible to stay in balance." Every athlete and military warrior knows the importance of this principle.

Deploy with the Right Mindset implies starting with the right stance to maximize your chances of staying in balance when the unexpected occurs. Certainly this makes sense in physical endeavors, but it is even more important in the mental, emotional, and spiritual dimensions. What does this look like?

A vignette from the life of King Jehosophat of Judah comes to mind. You can read the full account in 2 Chronicles, Chapter 20. Using New King James Version (NKJV) Bible excerpts below, my condensed version goes like this: Three foreign armies, "a great multitude" were closing in on Judah and its capitol, Jerusalem. Recognizing the likelihood of disaster "sword, judgment, pestilence, famine," King Jehosophat was fearful and sought the Lord (*no kidding!*)

Then a man of great courage and conviction in the Spirit of the Lord, Jahaziel (a grandson of Benaniah who we will talk more about in the next chapter; for now, he was one of David's mighty men who killed a lion in a pit on a snowy day... *that* family had backbone!), boldly proclaimed to the leaders and to the King himself, "Do not be afraid or dismayed because of this great multitude, for the battle is not yours, but God's." King Jehosophat takes the counsel to heart and chooses an interesting formation for the battle, putting the praise singers out in front. Bottom Line: "The Lord set ambushes..." and the invaders fell to their own swords of fratricide, killing one another to the last man. Judah was saved, God was glorified, and there was rest all around for the nation of Judah.

This has *everything* to do with resilience! Look at this through mental, emotional, and spiritual lenses. Deploying with the Right Mindset alludes to an ongoing state of mind, a positive outlook that must be renewed continuously. It is about an optimistic stance that gives strength as one waits and trusts in the Lord. In Christian vernacular, this implies a spirit of praise, an "attitude of gratitude."

Whether one is going into battle with a nursery full of two year olds, or crossing the Line of Departure (LD) from Kuwait into Iraq, having a spirit of praise, an attitude of gratitude, makes a huge difference in spiritual strength and resiliency. Recall the thesis fundamental to the Posttraumatic Growth concepts discussed in Chapter 3, namely, "One's mindset going into trauma heavily influences the way one views trauma, and predisposes them to become either bitter or better."

This healthy mental, emotional, and spiritual stance does not come naturally. How do we get into this right mindset, spiritually, that is? Certainly there are basics which are key. Regarding basics, Willie Mays, a famous All Star baseball player in the 1950s and 60s, was asked by a reporter about his secret of success. His response: "They throw the ball, I hit it. They hit the ball, I catch it." These are the basics: hitting and catching, blocking and tackling, jabbing and hooking, falling and getting back up. (http://www.baseball-almanac.com/quotes/quomays.shtml)

As a young spiritual warrior, I learned about spiritual basics from great mentors, like the Seidels and so many others. They taught me about the fundamentals: Worship, Bible Study, Prayer, Fellowship with other believers, Scripture memory, Journaling, and helping others benefit from the knowledge and relevance of Jesus in their daily lives. Each of these spiritual basics help to form a mindset such as described in Romans 12:2 (underline emphasis added), "And do not be conformed to this world, but be <u>transformed by the renewing of your mind</u>, so that you may prove what the will of God is, that which is good and acceptable and perfect."

There is another specific technique that helps me deploy with the right mindset. It's music. Yes, I admit it! A tough Airborne Ranger infantry dude who recognizes the power of music, especially inspirational Christian music which points one upward and onward, especially music that has been prepared and assembled ahead of time, music that will comfort you in your deepest needs and your most agonizing hurts.

This explains the Resilience Playlist selections that are salted throughout the Bounce Builder sections in *Resilience God Style.* The Resilience Playlist comprises a selection of key stress busters, mood changers, and praise songs which can help you spiritually achieve the right mindset, the right attitude. Along with other spiritual disciplines we have discussed, this playlist tool can greatly help you kick-start your day or regain the right spiritual, mental, and emotional bearings when you are knocked off balance.

Before the fight such a musical tool highlighting God's Word is encouraging and comforting, helping one maintain the right balance and mindset. *After* you have been wounded, traumatized by whatever makes your day, these old friends are often the least intrusive means to help you have a praise reflex, a grateful rejoinder, a growth response.

The Resilience Playlist has been a powerful tool in helping me respond positively to my own traumas of life. As well, I have seen powerful results with wounded warriors who may not have the ability or inclination to read their Bible, or talk about "Jesus things," greatly benefiting from the comfort and encouragement of Christian music. It helps heal their wounded hearts, minds, and souls. As our Infantry Sergeant would say again, "This stuff really works! Hooah!"

A final question regarding this ounce of prevention: "Are you doing everything possible to prepare for a positive response, a Godly response, to the trauma on your horizon? How about music? Do you have a Resilience Playlist? Are these songs your 'friends'?" When the tsunami rolls in it will be too late to pull it all together. Compile your list and make it part of your equipment now.

Develop and Rehearse "Actions on Contact" (Get Ready!)

Kathleen and I were enjoying a pretty drive along Highway 29 (named after the famed 29th Infantry Division of WWII) toward Lynchburg, Virginia. It is also a route many a Civil War soldier knew well, particularly those present at the sober surrender at Appomattox.

We had a Christian song playing ("Just Give Me Jesus" by Jeremy Camp), the trees arched over the highway forming a cool corridor on a hot summer day. You get the picture—a pleasant moment enjoying good music, the beauty of God's creation, and time with the love of your life.

Kathleen then nonchalantly commented about the song: "I want that played at my funeral." Although it initially felt like a splash of cold water, I recognized that her comment was simply reflecting on the glorious day when she would join her Lord and Savior for eternity. Prayerfully, it will be several decades hence before we play that song, but Kathleen in essence was helping us develop what the military would call "Actions on Contact," those dance steps that military units establish, train, and rehearse for when they initially encounter the inevitable and unpredictable twists and turns of the battlefield, particularly the highly vulnerable times when they have a "first contact" with the enemy. What happens if we get hit with artillery? What about a sniper? An IED? What if we have wounded soldier who needs to be evacuated from the battlefield?

So it is with us all as warriors on the journey of life. We must consider the "Actions on Contact" that we can develop ahead of time, to increase the likelihood of resilient responses to the reality of trauma in our lives. What do we do when the body slam occurs, when we are extremely vulnerable, perhaps disillusioned, disoriented, hurt, betrayed, asking, "Why?"

While we all seek to keep a good stance and stay balanced, we will periodically get knocked down to the canvas for the various reasons we have discussed: consequences of our own sinfulness or that of others, unexplainable natural disasters, and unseen war in the spiritual realm. Archibald Signorelli stated in *Plan of Creation or Sword of Truth*, published in 1916, "We Fall the Way We Lean." This chapter has discussed how to lean in the right direction, particularly spiritually, so that we also fall in the right direction, in the direction of resilience and restoration. Our next chapter addresses the second phase of the Resilience Life Cycle©. Chapter 6, "Weathering the Storm" discusses specific actions on contact that trained and resilient warriors will reflexively take when they know that they have taken a hit.

We have emphasized:

- Know Your Calling
- Know Your Enemy
- Know Your Friends
- Know Your Equipment
- Deploy with the Right Mindset
- Develop and Rehearse "Actions on Contact" (Get Ready!)

Application of these preventive steps will truly be the "ounce of prevention worth a pound of cure." They will build bounce for you and for me.

> Application of these preventive steps: Know Your Calling, Know Your Enemy, Know Your Friends, Know Your Equipment, Deploy with the Right Mindset, and Develop and Rehearse "Actions on Contact" will truly be the "ounce of prevention worth a pound of cure."

See the *Resilience God Style Study Guide* "BEFORE" section to develop personal applications for the principles contained in this chapter.

BOUNCE BUILDERS:

1. Coy, Colonel Jimmie Dean. *Prisoners of Hope: A Gathering of Eagles, Book Three.* Mobile, AL. Evergreen, 2005.
2. Ruth, Peggy Joyce. *Psalm 91: God's Shield of Protection.* Military ed. Kirkwood, MO: Impact Christian Book, 2005.
3. Willey, Barry E. *Out of the Valley.* Ft. Worth, TX: Creative Team Publishing, 2016.
4. New Song. "Sheltering Trees," as recorded in *Sheltering Tree.* Nashville: Benson Records, 2004.
5. Lees, Robin. "We Will Stand," as recorded in *Love Jesus.* Birdland Productions, Inc., 1999.
6. Harris, Larnelle. He Strength of the Lord," as recorded in *The Best of 10 Years, Vol. 2.* Nashville: Benson Records, 1994.

ADDITIONAL STUDY:

1. Barton, Ruth Hayley. *Strengthening the Soul of Your Leadership: Seeking God in the Crucible of Ministry.* Downers Grove, IL: InterVarsity Press/IVP Boooks, 2008
2. Jackson Jr., Harry R. *The Warrior's Heart: Rules of Engagement for the Spiritual War Zone.* Chosen Books, 2004.
3. Self, Nate. *Two Wars: One Hero's Fight on Two Fronts—Abroad and Within.* Carol Stream, IL: Tyndale House, 2008.

6

Weathering the Storm

"At intervals between a bomb falling it sounded like church: voices from nearby slit trenches all chanting the Lord's prayer together—over and over again. Louder when the bombs hit closer."–Veteran Army Air Forces Bombadier and Olympic runner Louie Zamperini, recounting the Japanese bombardment of U.S. forces at Funafuti Atoll in World War II, as recorded in *Unbroken* by Laura Hillenbrand, page 117.

The book *Unbroken* is an amazing life story of resilience. It depicts Louie Zamperini enduring and overcoming some of the worst situations life has to offer: smashed Olympic dreams, gut-wrenching combat resulting in personal wounds and loss of trusted comrades, survival at sea in a failing life raft with sharks brushing past, torture by sadistic Japanese captors, and postwar disillusion and dysfunction. *Unbroken* is truly an inspiring story of "weathering the storm," resisting horrendous conditions, and bouncing back to be better and stronger after the storm passes.

It's also a story of faith: the simple and desperate faith of a man on the brink of death in combat which grows into a profound spiritual transformation of one trapped in the despair of post-traumatic stress, alcoholism, and post-war relational dysfunction. Louie Zamperini, along with so many other warriors in "the greatest generation," is a true profile in resilience, and an apt illustration of the relevance of spirituality and faith to the Resilience Life Cycle©. His life particularly instructs and inspires us regarding how to "weather the storms" that life sends our way.

The Bible also has much to offer the wounded warrior, or the "Gold Star Mother" who has lost her son to combat, the struggling businessman, the unsuspecting cancer victim, and so many others who are suddenly beset by trauma and tribulation. The Bible doesn't sugarcoat these realities. It tells the stories of people who are just like us; their stories are just like ours.

> The Bible tells the stories of people who are just like us,
> their stories are just like ours.

Consider the Warrior David's lament (Psalm 55:4-8) which highlights what today we would call post-traumatic stress and combat trauma (underlined emphasis added):

"My <u>heart is in anguish</u> within me,
And the <u>terrors of death</u> have fallen upon me.
<u>Fear and trembling</u> come upon me,
And <u>horror</u> has overwhelmed me.

I said, 'Oh that I had wings like a dove!
I would <u>fly away and be at rest</u>.
Behold, I would wander far away,
I would lodge in the wilderness.
I would <u>hasten to my place of refuge</u>
From the stormy wind and tempest.'"

When the storms roll into our lives, we have "anguished hearts" like David and we want to flee the pain, the agony, the reality of trauma and tribulation in our lives. Like David we want to "fly away and be at rest...and hasten to our place of refuge from the stormy wind and tempest."

But trauma does not bend to easy solutions. It does not provide a simple means of escape. Trauma is real and it hurts, but God knows, and understands, and becomes our refuge and strength in the midst of our trauma. Consider Psalm 46:1-3 (italics added): "God is our refuge and strength, *a very present help in trouble*. Therefore we will not fear, though the earth should change and though the mountains slip into the heart of the sea; though its waters roar and foam, though the mountains quake at its swelling pride."

Also consider Jesus and his disciples afloat in a small boat amidst a raging storm on the Sea of Galilee (Matthew 8:23-27). This great storm, like so many on that sea, rose suddenly. Jesus was sleeping through all the commotion. The disciples were terrified and fearful of death, "Save us, Lord; we are perishing!" Christ rebukes the disciples for their "little faith" and then rebukes the winds and the sea, calming the storm. He demonstrates that a Sovereign God is with them and can save them (and us) in and through the very real trials in the present and for eternity. Christ was also teaching them (and us) that faith is essential, making all the difference as we weather the perilous and uncontrollable storms in our own lives. We see this in the life of combat veterans such as Louie Zamperini and on each page of the Bible.

> Faith is essential. It makes all the difference as we weather the perilous and uncontrollable storms in our own lives.

Having discussed "Building Bounce" in Chapter 5, we now turn to "Weathering the Storm" as we continue to advance our understanding of the Resilience Life Cycle©, shown below as a reminder.

RESILIENCE LIFE CYCLE©

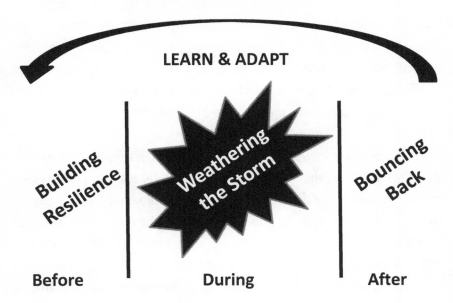

We will provide five specific ways to spiritually "Weather the Storm."

1. Call 911
2. Start the IV
3. Keep Breathing
4. Draw from Your Well of Courage
5. Remember Your Calling

Call 911

NOTE: Your first call may *actually* be to the emergency number, 911, to request immediate medical care or support from police or fire personnel. For many, such an emergency call will not be warranted, yet other types of "911 calls" will be absolutely essential.

- *Pray to God*. Unashamedly cry out to Him. In the case of severe trauma or danger this often happens spontaneously as the created one reaches out in desperation to their Creator. Such prayer need not be highly sophisticated—it's simply honest and real communication with the living God. In the example of Louie Zamperini, a spiritual neophyte in his early days of combat, prayer was somewhat awkward, yet a very present help in trouble:

  "The two-week mark (on a life raft in the Pacific Ocean in a seemingly hopeless situation) was a different kind of turning point for Louie. He began to pray aloud. He had no how to speak to God, so he recited snippets of prayers that he'd heard in movies. Phil (Louie's pilot and deeply religious friend, shot down together in their bomber) bowed his head as Louie spoke, offering "Amen" at the end. Mac (the bomber's tail gunner who became hopeless and died during the ordeal) only listened." (*Unbroken*, page 156; parenthetical comments provided for context.)

Certainly it is easier to communicate with someone that you talk to frequently. A pre-trauma prayer ethic (an indicator of spiritual fitness), richly fueled by a knowledge of God's scriptural assurances of provision and protection for His children, allows for even more effective and powerful communication with God when the storm rolls in. Philippians 4:6, 7 (parenthetical comments added) summarizes it this way: "Be anxious for nothing, but in everything by prayer and supplication with thanksgiving, let your requests be made known to God. And the peace of God which passes all understanding will guard your hearts (emotional protection) and minds (mental protection) in Christ Jesus."

- *Ask for help from your most trusted family and friends*. If you have developed true "relational fitness," characterized in part by deep relationships of trust and vulnerability, you will know who this small number of family and friends is. It is useful to have "rehearsed" this ahead of time. Who are these folks? Although really close friends may know this implicitly, are you sure they know who they are? When hearing "the news," some will pray, some will call to simply affirm you, some will offer wise counsel (not like Job's friends who initially offered condemnation and premature solutions); some will jump on airplanes to be with you, to sit and pray, fix meals, read scripture to you, listen, and cry. You have been there for them; now they will be there for you.

- *In addition to your strong relational "inner circle," ask for help from "professionals" you trust.* Maybe this is the chaplain, the pastor or counselor at your church or another church, or a professional in the community. These people are generally competent and caring, aware of the resources and immediate actions to help "triage" your wounded heart, soul, and emotions.

- *Accept help from others with a heart to help.* Robert Nuttall, a Gulf War veteran who suffered from PTSD and TBI, and his wife, Amy, introduced in Chapter 1, tell the story of a local church they had never visited that had a huge impact in their early days of shock, confusion, and healing. Like clock- work, church members would bring a meal each evening, expecting nothing in return. No gospel tracts, no ulterior motives—just the love of Jesus. This church later became their source of spiritual comfort and healing.

> Like clockwork, church members would bring a meal each evening, expecting nothing in return.

Start the IV

IV refers to *intravenous*, a medical procedure used to bypass a damaged or dysfunctional gastrointestinal tract to provide nutrients and healing drugs into the bloodstream and to the point of need. An IV is also used as a lifesaving measure to assist with physically traumatized patients who need a rapid infusion to stabilize their medical condition.

An incident from the annals of "Rakkasan" history (187th Regimental Combat Team, now part of the 101st Airborne Division at Fort Campbell, Kentucky) illustrates this practice. The setting is the Rakkasan Change of Command in October 1994. Colonel Bob Dees is turning over the regiment to Colonel Bill Martinez. After an intense and hot day of rehearsals the day before, the 3,000+ Rakkasans, including supporting artillery, engineers, signal, and other members of the combined arms team are arrayed on the Fort Campbell parade field with the three story banner of "Old Abe," the distinctive 101st Airborne Screaming Eagle, looking down on the impressive ceremony. One of the Rakkasan troopers, no doubt dehydrated from the previous day's rehearsals and that morning's tough PT (physical training) routine, collapses in formation. Those to the right and left in formation quietly help the fallen comrade, while medics positioned in the rear infiltrate the formation, trying to avoid notice by the large audience in the reviewing stand. Arriving at the site of the fallen soldier, the medics quickly insert an

IV needle with tubing attached to a bag of saline solution to stem the onset of heat exhaustion or, even worse, heat stroke.

Just as the medics are getting ready to escort the fallen soldier to a shady location behind the formation, the Commander of Troops shouts "Pass in Review," the command for all the troop formations to parade past the reviewing party and the thousands gathered in the stands. In true Rakkasan fashion, fellow comrades snatch the soldier to his feet and place the IV bag of saline solution, still attached to the tubing and needle in the soldier's arm, on the end of the soldier's M16 rifle. Within seconds the soldier's infantry battalion commander directs "Right turn, March." Off goes the formation with the Rakkasan soldier marching in ranks with the IV bag on his weapon, now a badge of honor marking him as a resilient warrior. Although this incident is somewhat humorous and illustrative of a strong warrior ethic, it also demonstrates the essence of the resilience process: falling down, getting assistance, and getting back up to continue the mission. Without the IV, the soldier could not continue and was at risk of more serious injury or death. With the IV, the soldier was soon able to bounce back.

When we go through gut-wrenching traumas, when we are "weathering the storm," the rapid and concentrated IV intake of God's Word is critical. Psalm 57:1 says, "And in the shadow of your wings I will take refuge until destruction passes by." Taking refuge in the shadow of God's wings takes many forms, but it absolutely includes a continuous flow of God's encouraging and enriching Word directly into our heart, soul, and spirit. More specifically, one must go far past the normal daily, sustaining devotionals lasting minutes, to extended hours and even days of concentrated soaking in God's Word; in prayer, reflection, and praise (not *for* the situation, but *in* the situation, expressing the confidence that God remains loving and sovereign).

> When we are "weathering the storm," the rapid and concentrated IV intake of God's Word is critical.

In times of trauma, such as when Kathleen and I lost our first child, Amy, just before birth, I have found it imperative to allow God to "Make me lie down in green pastures" (fresh, verdant, restorative) and "Lead me beside quiet waters" (away from the roar of sirens, and the roar of my own doubts and pain) in order to *"restore my soul and guide me* in the paths of righteousness for His name's sake." (Psalm 23:2, 3; parenthetical comments added). This entire process of restoring our soul begins as we "mainline" the Word of God by reading it ourselves, having others read it to us, and hearing it on audio and in song.

Psalm 119:11-16 summarizes the point succinctly (underline emphasis added):

> " [11] Your word I have treasured in my heart,
> That I may not sin against You.
> [12] Blessed are You, O LORD; Teach me Your statutes.
> [13] With my lips I have told of
> All the ordinances of Your mouth.

[14] I have rejoiced in the way of Your testimonies,
As much as in all riches.
[15] I will meditate on Your precepts
And regard Your ways.
[16] I shall delight in Your statutes;
I shall not forget Your word."

When we take incoming and suffer wounds, we as spiritually fit and resilient warriors must reflexively go to God's Word and IV the invaluable riches which await us there.

Keep Breathing

In my many emergency treatment classes over years in the military, the acronym "ABC" was a common denominator, reminding me (and others) about **A**irway, **B**reathing, and **C**irculation. We were told the first critical step is to "Clear the Airway" to allow the patient to keep breathing. So it is in a spiritual sense. To the best of your ability, *keep doing what you know to do*: keep breathing, follow your training. Spiritually fit and resilient warriors will reflexively continue to exercise spiritual disciplines. These will include devotional times, prayer, spiritual reflection, and journaling. They will continue to apply physical disciplines like eating, exercise, and rest as ways to deal with the storm surge of stress, uncertainty, and anguish.

> Spiritually fit and resilient warriors will reflexively continue to exercise spiritual disciplines.

- *Count your way.* In the Airborne, the paratrooper who has just jumped out of the airplane is trained to count from one to four ("one thousand, two thousand...") in a reflexive way to keep their mind in gear, avoid fear responses, and execute emergency measures if the main parachute doesn't open. This technique of "counting your way" (continuing to breathe) through the first seconds, minutes, and days of a devastating, challenging, fearful, or life changing experience is critical when you have just suffered a physical, mental, spiritual, emotional, or relational train wreck. It is the first step in a right and resilient response to trauma. From my early days as a lieutenant of infantry, I was often reminded by senior commanders "We fight the way we train." Over the years, I found this maxim to be absolutely true. Similarly, each of us also responds to trauma and crisis the way we train.

- *Practice "spiritual breathing."* The founder of Campus Crusade for Christ, Dr. Bill Bright, developed a concept called "spiritual breathing." This practice consists of "exhaling" the impurities (sin, doubt, venom from others, et al.) and "inhaling" the indwelling presence of God's Holy Spirit in obedience to scriptural exhortation to "be filled with the Spirit" (Ephesians 5:18, which in the original Greek means "Keep being filled with the Spirit"). In addition to this useful discipline of spiritual breathing, the broader admonition to Keep Breathing in every aspect of our spiritual lives is important to weathering the storm.

- *Hit a knee.* Think of the 280-pound defensive end who has just been body-slammed on the football field, he's had the wind knocked out of him and he's a bit groggy. It is not considered unmanly for this gladiator to come out of the game for a play or two, *hit a knee* as the expression goes, regain his breath, and then later rejoin the team on the field to the applause of the stadium fans for his courage to bounce back and fight again. Coaches and players alike appreciate that it would be unwise for this traumatized player to continue without a short break, subjecting him to further injury and creating vulnerability in the team's performance.

    The same holds true for wounded warriors on any battlefield of life. It is not only okay to admit we are wounded and we need help; it is the wise way to get fixed and get back into the fight. Particularly in today's military, the "stigma" against admitting need and asking for help is a significant detriment to the proper identification and healing of the wounds of war, particularly those hidden wounds of the heart, soul, and spirit. Military leadership is working hard to remove such stigma, real and perceived, which deter troops and their families from acknowledging their deepest needs.

- *Record the journey.* As a part of the "Before" spiritual disciplines, if you have developed a consistent ethic of journaling, you will reflexively continue this process. Your journal becomes a very personal and intimate way to cry out to God in writing. Many times when the shock of trauma locks up our emotions and injects doubt about foundational values, the practice of journaling or recording the journey becomes useful therapy and a practical way to reassert faith and objective truth when the ground is shaking beneath us.

As a repository of life experiences and "God moments," our journal also becomes a timely reminder of God's love, grace, and provision in our past which provides encouragement and hope for the present and the future. Were my house to suddenly burst into flames today, the prized possessions I would seek to escape with would be my Bible and my journals in which I have recorded literally decades of life experiences seen through the lens of God's Holy Spirit, the truth of His Word, and the person of Jesus.

Draw from Your Well of Courage

September 29, 2008—the Dow Jones Industrial Average loses 777 points, signaling a financial freefall that would last not days, but months. In early October 2008, I was sitting in a Time Out Conference in Monterey, California, attended by many influential leaders from Silicon Valley and beyond. During each session, the assorted smart phones and mobile devices would scream as the markets fell off another cliff to an even lower precipice. Executives would rush out of the room to triage financial holdings for themselves and the clients they served. The pervasive sentiment was *fear*—fear about loss of revenues and lifestyle, fear about loss of reputation and trust, fear about the future. Unavoidably all conversations, including presentations from the conference speakers, turned to the reality of fear in these businessmen's lives and how they might have courage in this "perfect financial storm."

As a military man who has faced many daunting crises, I reminded the group that courage is not the absence of fear. Courage is the ability to overcome fear to accomplish a daunting task, honorably to the best of your ability. The question then is how to courageously overcome fear in the first moments and days of trauma and crisis.

God provided a simple equation in those days of financial catastrophe: FEAR + FAITH = COURAGE. So it is in every endeavor of life, with FAITH as the "secret sauce" for so many of us. This faith has many components which fuel our wells of courage, our reservoirs of resilience. Most important is ultimate faith in God, as we previously discussed Jesus calming the raging storm for his frightful disciples who needed *more faith in God's sovereignty* and willing- ness and capacity to protect them in and through the storm.

The Book of Hebrews helps us better describe this kind of faith as an antidote to fear: "Therefore, <u>do not throw away your *confidence*</u>, which has a great reward. For you have <u>need of *endurance*</u>, so that when you have done the will of God, you may receive what is promised." After emphasizing "the righteous shall live by faith," the writer continues, "But we are not of those who shrink back to destruction, but of those who have faith to the *preserving of the soul.* Now faith is the *assurance* of things hoped for, the *conviction* of things not seen." (Hebrews 10:35, 38, 39; 11:1, italics added) Faith in God truly does provide resilient warriors with confidence, endurance, soul preservation, assurance, conviction, and overall courage.

Faith and confidence in self are also important as we remember the reflexes and confidence that airborne training produces. An equally critical ingredient is *faith in others*, the result of teambuilding and shared hardship under previous challenges.

> Faith in God does provide resilient warriors with confidence, endurance, soul preservation, assurance, conviction, and overall courage.

A final element is obtaining *faith from others*, drawing courage and inspiration from the examples of fellow warriors. As a first reference, Hebrews 11 reminds us of inspiring characters of courage and faith of such as Abraham, Sarah, Joseph, Moses, Rahab, Gideon, David, and many others; a veritable hall of fame for faithful heroes. As further inspiration, we are reminded that these "warriors" per- formed mighty acts in faith even though, [37]"They were stoned, they were sawn in two, they were tempted, they were put to death with the sword; they went about in sheepskins, in goatskins, being destitute, afflicted, ill-treated [38](*men* of whom the world was not worthy), wandering in deserts and mountains and caves and holes in the ground.[39] And all these, having gained approval through their faith, did not receive what was promised..." (Hebrews 11: 37 – 39, underlined emphasis added).

Hebrews 12 continues this progression, highlighting Jesus as the "author and perfecter of faith, who for the joy set before Him, endured the cross, despising the shame, and has sat down at the right hand of the throne of God. For consider Him who has endured such hostility by sinners against Himself, so that you will not grow weary and lose heart." Now that is faith. That is courage. *That* is *resilience*.

> Such biblical examples are tremendously encouraging when we are tempted to feel alone in our storm.

Similarly, personal relationships with people of faith and valor, along with great biographical accounts of faith and courage will supply our well of courage during times of weathering the storm. For starters I point you to the movies, books, Medal of Honor citations, and songs recommended in our Bounce Builders.

Remember Your Calling

Remembering the story of Jacob Calloway and his tragic incident in Afghanistan (Chapter 5), the last piece of advice I gave to his inquiring mother was, "Tell Jacob not to question his call. He is a soldier in a noble and honorable profession that defends the innocent and rescues the downtrodden from the ugly jaws of evil. This is a tough situation, but it is not his fault. We will all get through this together. We have lots of important work to do in the future." So it is with each of us. Remembering the noble purposes that we have dedicated our lives to, becomes an important anchor for our soul and vector for our future, an important ingredient that helps us maintain hope and direction amidst crisis.

We have covered the basics of *weathering the storm:*

1. Call 911
2. Start the IV
3. Keep Breathing
4. Draw from Your Well of Courage
5. Remember Your Calling

One of the most poignant examples of people "weathering the storm" are Gold Star Parents (having lost their military son in combat) Sharon and Deacon Collins, both retired Army lieutenant colonels with 42 years of combined service. They kindly provided their story, knowing that it will encourage and equip others who experience similar "body slams" in their lives. Their son, Robert Wilson Collins, was the first graduate from the United States Military Academy (USMA) Class of 2008 to be killed in combat. (Robert's West Point Eulogy page can be seen at http://www.west-point.org/users/usma2008/64279.)

In essence, Robert was an All-American boy and then some— varsity athlete in multiple sports, talented Spanish linguist, gifted trumpet player, President of his high school class for three years, an industrious part-time sales associate for several businesses, and an active humanitarian in his church and his community. Although these accomplishments by this talented young man are impressive, Robert's greatest distinction was his mark as a man of principle and conviction who had a huge heart for others. Understandably, his parents loved their only son dearly.

While Robert had not planned on a military career, he changed course when he saw the tragedies that occurred in our nation on September 11, 2001, and the ensuing Global War on Terror. He made a decision to serve his nation in the military and was accepted to West Point. After a successful cadet career and graduation in May 2008, Robert went through the Infantry Basic Officer Leadership Course (IBOLC), as well as Ranger School. In a particularly meaningful ceremony at his Airborne School graduation, Robert's mother, Lieutenant Colonel Sharon Collins, U.S. Army, Retired, proudly pinned her own Airborne wings (received when she was the honor graduate of Airborne School in 1977) on her son's chest. Robert's military service was clearly a family affair by this point in time—a time of joy, and accomplishment, and honor.

In October 2009 Robert deployed with the Army's famed Third Infantry Division (3ID), the "Marne Division" so nicknamed because of their World War I heroics along the Marne River in France. The division was engaged in Operation Iraqi Freedom in northern Iraq. On April 7, 2010, First Lieutenant (1LT) Robert Collins' three vehicle convoy was attacked by an IED (improvised explosive device) in Mosul, Iraq. His vehicle, traveling in the middle of the column, was catapulted over a football field distance by the explosive force. Robert was killed along with his vehicle driver, Specialist William Anthony Blount from Petal, Mississippi. Miraculously, the five soldiers in the rear of Robert's vehicle survived, largely because Robert as their leader had insured they were properly wearing the "Marne standard" (the required protective gear specified for 3ID soldiers).

Robert's loss was honored and grieved by his 3ID comrades, his West Point classmates, his church and community, his extended family, his beloved sweetheart of many years Nicolle Williams, and so many others across this land. The dedications and expressions of support to the family have been overwhelming: the "1LT Robert Collins" U.S. Post Office in Tyrone, Georgia; the Patriot Field House at Sandy Creek High School in memory of Robert; the dedication of USMA Cadet Field Training 2010 as "Task Force Collins;" and many, many others. Robert was fittingly honored as a "Fallen Hero" on Headline News' Nancy Grace show, October 12, 2011.

Most of all, Robert's parents Deacon and Sharon honored and grieved the loss of their only beloved son, and they still do. They will never forget. Yet they serve as inspiration for each of us, models of resilience under the toughest of conditions.

Although the Collins' had lived the military life themselves, including dealing with the sensitivities of performing duties as an Army Survivor Assistance Officer (SAO) to assist those losing a loved one, it is different when it is your own son. This "knock on the door" came unexpectedly, as it always does. Woken from a dead sleep at 6 AM on April, 8, 2010, Deacon Collins looked out the window to see two men in uniform. He immediately knew. Deacon and Sharon quickly threw on clothes as they began to "weather the storm" that had just invaded their lives.

The Collins' calmly and graciously welcomed the Casualty Assistance Officer (CAO), a young Signal Corps captain charged with making the death notification, and the supporting Chaplain into their home. In the thoughts of Sharon Collins, "we will fall apart later...our world has changed forever...but we will meet this moment with grace." The visitors mouthed the words a military parent never wants to hear: "We regret to inform you that your son, First Lieutenant Robert Wilson Collins, has been killed in Iraq."

Sharon knew that faith, family, and friends would be the key to living through this nightmarish reality. After Robert deployed, Sharon had done "a dry run in her head," conditioning herself in case the unthinkable happened to Robert. When the fateful knock did come, she reflexively "started the faith IV" as she immediately asked the Chaplain for prayer. Instead of "shaking a fist at God," "Thy will be done" was a constant refrain in those early moments and days, representing a mindset to flee anger and bitterness. She "kept breathing" (referring to our earlier discussion regarding maintaining familiar routines) as she fixed coffee for their nervous visitors. Notifying "911 Friends" immediately, the Collins' were comforted by dear, trusted friends and neighbors who were hugging them within 15 minutes. Their Hopewell United Methodist Church friends likewise provided tangible sustaining support, just as earlier when men in the church had mentored Robert, preparing him spiritually for an uncertain future. As a "Stephen's Minister" at the church and participant in the women's group, Sharon had a healthy relational network that closed ranks to support the family.

> Faith, family, and friends are keys to living through nightmarish reality.

We are inspired by Robert's sacrifice as a "Fallen Hero," and equally inspired by these resilient Gold Star parents, Deacon and Sharon Collins. For them, Faith, Family, and Friends made the difference, all the difference. Having invested in resilience ahead of time, they weathered the loss of their dearly beloved son Robert through the power of faith, family, and friends. As they continue to bounce back, they will no doubt comfort many others with that which they have been comforted. They are true Resilient Warriors.

See the *Resilience God Style Study Guide* "DURING" section to develop personal applications for the principles contained in this chapter.

BOUNCE BUILDERS:

1. American Bible Society. *God Understands...When You Feel.* Series. 8 vols. (unnumbered). New York: American Bible Society, 2009.
2. Cash, Carey H. *A Table in the Presence.* Nashville: W Publishing Group, 2004.
3. Cook, Jane Hampton, Jocelyn Green and John Croushorn. *Battlefields & Blessings: Stories of Faith and Courage from the war in Iraq & Afghanistan.* Chattanooga, TN: God & Country, 2009.
4. Plekenpol, Chris. *Faith in the Fog of War.* Sisters, OR: Multnomah, 2006.
5. Gallegos, Nancy. "You Are My Hiding Place,: as contained in *Heaven's Glow.* Colorado Springs, CO: 2008.
6. Hopkins, Dave. "God is Our Refuge,: as contained in *Songs from the Ranch,* DH-04, © 2000 Lisa Hopkins.
7. Selah. "Hold On," as recorded in *Press On.* Nashville: Curb Records, 2001.

ADDITIONAL STUDY:

1. Hillenbrand, Laura. *Unbroken.* New York: Random House, 2010.
2. Lueders, Beth J. *Lifting Our Eyes: Finding God's Grace Through the Virginia Tech Tragedy; The Lauren McCain Story.* New York: Berkeley Books, 2007.
3. Shive, Dave. *Night Shift: God Works in the Dark Hours of Life.* Lincoln, NE: Back to the Bible, 2001.
4. Yancey, Philip. *Where Is God When It Hurts?* Grand Rapids: Zondervan, 1977.

7

Bouncing Back...
Without Getting Stuck!

"Okay, men, if there is anyone out there that needs to get unstuck, to bounce back, to lay down their baggage at the foot of the cross of Christ, then now is the time. You may have drug around an anchor for years—perhaps your combat memories, or lingering addictions, or bitterness about the woulda', coulda', shoulda' missed opportunities in life. You know what it is. Come forward now."

The silence was deafening. In the first few moments after an invitation for men to be vulnerable, to deal honestly with their need for transformation in the power of Christ, one never knows what the outcome will be. Maybe everyone will stay hunkered in their foxholes of life, isolated and hurting.

Then I saw him. Looking across the sizeable sanctuary of Thomas Road Baptist Church in Lynchburg, VA, I could see movement on the main aisle about 50 yards away at the very rear of the gathering. Instantly I saw the bright yellow flash on his baseball hat, with a diagonal black stripe. As an Army Veteran, I knew that this was the distinctive 1st Cavalry Division patch. With halting steps the man began to walk the aisle towards me. Then I noticed his white beard—no doubt a Vietnam Veteran. Soon other men also noticed the veteran limping slowly down the aisle— "you can do it... proud of you man... thanks for your service." At one point about halfway, another man joined the weathered warrior coming forward for healing of his hidden wounds. The new companion was a pastor who lent physical and emotional support for this veteran's most significant steps in his life since he left the jungles of Vietnam.

Now 5,000 men are on their feet, cheering wildly. As this warrior fights tears and collapse, he presses through the last ten yards to the front of the inspired throng of men. I meet him at the foot of the stage; we share a bear hug as he weeps uncontrollably, releasing years of emotional baggage and sensing a new hope. He falls to his knees and cries out to God, "Jesus help me. I need to get unstuck. I need to move on. I commit my life fully to you. Thank you for loving me, for forgiving me, and for saving me from the painful memories that have haunted me for decades. I lay it all down before you, Lord. Thank you! Thank you!"

Thus began a new life.

And then the flood gates broke. The next man to come forward whispered in my ear, "You know, Sir. I was a Marine sniper... and a good one. (I knew what this young man was telling me.) I don't see how God could ever forgive me for what I have done." After a simple explanation that God loved him and honored his selfless service as a warrior, the Marine simply said, "You know, I never looked at it that way." He then asked God's forgiveness and received in his heart the conviction that "...neither death, nor life, nor angels, nor principalities, nor things present, nor things to come, nor powers, nor height, nor depth, nor any other created thing, (and I might add *nor the spiritual, mental, and emotional challenges of being a Marine sniper in war*) will be able to separate us from the love of God, which is in Christ Jesus our Lord." (Romans 8:38, 39). The next day this Marine gave powerful testimony that indicated he had loosened his grip on guilt and false guilt, he understood and received God's love and forgiveness, he was ready to move forward with God and with life.

These responses and more were the results of asking a simple question: "Are you a tennis ball or an egg?" We had given a live demonstration—the splattered egg residue was everywhere, including on the Harley that was on stage as a prop. Conversely, the tennis ball bounced high, again and again. When I threw it into the audience, the men jumped to catch it as though it was Hank Aaron's 755th home run (beating Babe Ruth's former career home run record). No doubt that tennis ball is displayed proudly on some man's mantle. No one took the egg home. It was too messy.

Many of the men that night were resilient, spiritually fit warriors; yet many had been splattered like the egg. Some were clearly committed to building resilience for future storms in life, others were weathering storms in the present, some were in the process of bouncing back, and some were downright "stuck" in the mire of bitterness, the muck of failed relationships and shattered dreams, and the misery of a seemingly worthless past and a hopeless future. For all, bouncing back was an incredibly relevant topic.

After seeing the tennis ball and egg comparison, as well as understanding anew the biblical principles related to resilience, the men readily agreed that the best of all worlds is to bounce high like the tennis ball, ideally even higher than before in the power of Christ. Their life experiences also illustrated that it was easy to get stuck in the often lengthy process of bouncing back.

Bouncing back is the most dangerous phase of the resilience journey. "Building Bounce" on sunny days before the storm hits is hard work, and "Weathering the Storm" is very painful for a short and intense time when comforters are usually gathered about. "Bouncing Back" is the most dangerous and the most challenging. This process takes the longest, it is often the loneliest path, and it is fraught with many landmines (potential sticking points) along the way.

Hence, we devote our next two chapters to this "Bouncing Back" phase of The Resilience Life Cycle©. We will include commentary on how to get unstuck when the traumas of life have bogged us down for months, years, or decades.

> Bouncing back
> is the most dangerous phase of the resilience journey.

Jeff Manion describes the "Land Between" as "that space where we feel lost or lonely or deeply hurt—it is *fertile ground for our spiritual transformation* and for God's grace to be revealed in magnificent ways... The wilderness where faith can thrive is the very desert where it can dry up and die if we are not watchful." (*The Land Between*, page 19) In this meaningful book for those navigating the transitions that inevitably accompany trauma, he uses the wanderings of the nation of Israel as a laboratory to analyze the challenges of transition that we all face. In essence, each of us must navigate the "Land Between" as we move through the "Bouncing Back" phase. Discussing "The Blessing of the Land Between," Jeff Manion further states, page 192 (underline emphasis added), "*Pain is purposeful* when we respond to God with open and receptive hearts in the midst of deep trial. God intends to grow something beautiful and deep and lasting, but we must cooperate with God for the season of hardship to work its intended transformation. *Don't let your detour go wasted.* You are in training, and God is up to something good."

What did this process of bouncing back, this "Land Between," look like for Allen Clark, Vietnam Veteran, successful banker, distinguished leader in the Department of Veterans Affairs, founder of the Combat Faith ministry to veterans (http://www.combatfaith.com), and author of *Wounded Soldier, Healing Warrior*, a personal story of a Vietnam Veteran who lost his legs, but found his soul? While you should read this book for yourself, a few snapshots of Allen's story illustrate some points which are now becoming "common denominators" in this process of bouncing back. For starters, Allen experienced inexplicable loss in his life: the loss of his two legs, and the shattering of dreams for the future. Allen did manage a brave and optimistic spin in his initial letter home to his Dad (a distinguished veteran himself):

"As it stands now, my left leg has been amputated just below the knee, and it's questionable at the present to me about the right one. I will probably require more surgery in the States. It may be as long as eight or nine months before I'll be out of the hospital. *As far as I'm concerned, everything will be the same in the future*. The only difference is that I'll have to be fitted with prosthesis." (Allen's Letter to his Dad on June 18, 1967, the day after his wounds, page 19, *Wounded Soldier, Healing Warrior*)

Benefitting from forty years of life experience after enduring the many surgeries, the emotional trauma, the fourteen week commitment to the closed psychiatric ward of Brooke Army Hospital, and the significant life impacts (both obstacles and opportunities); Allen states the reality later in his book, page 30: "The events of June 17, 1967, resulted in *monumental changes to my life*." But, because of faith, family, and friends (such as spiritual mentors Andy and Gail Seidel, and so many others), the monumental changes had become catalysts for a powerful life transformation.

In his own words, Allen stated to me that "the resiliency after six years of psychiatrist appointments and anti-depressants occurred when Jesus, who had been Savior of my life, also became Lord because I began to understand prayer and the spiritual warfare battle in which I had been engaged for six years." In the words of 2 Corinthians 4:8,9, Allen Clark had certainly been afflicted, perplexed, and struck down, but because of his personal faith in Christ he was not crushed, despairing, forsaken, or destroyed. In God's Providence and Provision, Allen was able to grow as a resilient warrior, to truly rebound, and higher than ever before.

Allen puts it all in perspective in his book's conclusion (page 300): "If you have suffered and wondered why, Christ's love can heal your hurt and suffering and turn it into something positive and good just as He has done for me. *Without Him, My physical wounds may have healed, but my emotional wounds would not have. Most certainly, my heart would not have healed.* Without Him, I would not have become the man I am today. It is only through His sacrifice on the cross because of His unfailing love for me that I am alive and that I have been able to keep my sanity, raise a beautiful family, pursue a career, make a mark in life, develop a forgiving spirit, and put the horror of Vietnam behind me. His sacrifice for me was not in vain, and hits book is as much His story as it is mine."

> Aren't these the desired outcomes that we wish for every wounded warrior, inner healing as well as outer healing?

Isn't this where each of us would like to end up when we have been kicked in the gut, slammed to the ground, "beaten down" by life's unexpected and inexplicable twists? Allen's experience should inspire each of us to recognize that we can bounce back, in the power of faith, in the person of Jesus.

Equally inspiring is the story of Phil Downer, a former Marine machine gunner in Vietnam, a highly successful attorney, and now a popular speaker, author, and President of Discipleship Network of America (DNA) (http://www.dnaministries.org). Phil's compelling book, *From Hell to Eternity* is likewise a powerful account of rebounding from the seen and unseen wounds of war, to a "Life After Trauma," again because of faith, family, and friends. I also recommend this book (written with wife Susy, and children Paul and Anna Downer), as well as the Day of Discovery documentary which highlights Phil and other Downer family members in *The War Within: Finding Hope for Post-Traumatic Stress.* Phil Downer's story of the power of faith shines a bright light on the impacts felt and the reconciliation possible within a trauma sufferer's *family*.

He states, "This story is not just my own. It is also the story of my wife, Susy, and our six children... For Susy, the wounds I brought back from Vietnam made her the inadvertent target of ambush over and over again during the early years of our marriage. For Paul and Anna, the ups and downs of my journey as a man were also the dominant shaping forces of their childhoods. They grew up as the children of a wounded father, a Vietnam veteran suffering from Post-Traumatic Stress Disorder (PTSD). I went to war at the age of nineteen. They grew up in a post-war zone from the day they were born." (*From Hell to Eternity*, page 6)

Gratefully, God preserved this veteran and his family and has allowed them to have a voice into the lives of so many other troops, veterans, and their families. Faith made the real difference, allowing them to truly bounce, to rebound higher that anyone ever thought possible. This also is what we would hope for the 22 million veterans in our nation, the millions more of their family members, and our nation overall which continues to suffer the societal impacts of unresolved combat trauma. Likewise, this is our prayer for the four million troops who have served in the military since September 11, 2001 and the nearly two million who have personally deployed and experienced the traumas of war to varying degrees. This is also my prayer for you, whatever your "foxhole of life" may be at this moment.

> Faith makes the real difference,
> allowing those who have suffered, to truly bounce,
> to rebound higher than anyone ever thought possible.

What did these men and women have in common? Allen Clark, Phil Downer, Gary Beikirch and Lolly (the Vietnam Medal of Honor recipient and wife that we met in Chapter 3), Nate and Julie Self (the Ranger platoon leader we discussed in Chapter 5), Robert and Amy Nuttall (the couple who overcame PTSD and TBI in Chapter 1), as well as Sharon and Deacon Collins (the Gold Star Parents we met in Chapter 6), all experienced the horrors of war and resulting trauma to their bodies, minds, emotions, and their very souls. Yet, all bounced back in the power of personal faith. What common denominators, lessons learned, and biblical principles will instruct each of us in our recovery from the storms of life?

Let us cluster these into six categories, the first three (Chapter 7) focused on the past, with the last three (Chapter 8) focused on the future:

- Guard Your Primary Relationships
- Choose Forgiveness and Gratitude
- Grieve Well
- Sing a New Song
- Discern and Chart the Future
- Comfort Others

Guard Your Primary Relationships

The first dimension of Guard Your Primary Relationships is *press hard into God*, your most important relationship of all. Do not let your trauma drive your from your "first love" in Christ. Christ commended the church at Ephesus for their deeds and perseverance, but strongly admonished them for their apathy: "But I have *this* against you, that you have left your first love." (Revelation 2:4) In the next chapter of Revelation, similar words are directed toward the church at Laodicea: "I know your deeds, that you are neither cold nor hot; I wish you were cold or hot. So because you are lukewarm, and neither hot nor cold, I will spit you out of my mouth." (Revelation 3:15, 16) These exhortations to churches apply similarly to individual believers; we must not grow cold in our faith, we must not be lukewarm in our commitment, we must guard our "first love."

Allen Clark explains this dynamic: "When I went to Vietnam, I felt as if I grew closer to the Lord because I prayed more often— usually while under pressure, lonely for Jackie, or when in need or hurting. The isolation and loneliness of the war made me seek out comfort often, and I soon began attending chapel in Vietnam whenever I could. I continued to seek comfort from God while recovering from my wounds in the hospital in San Antonio. *However, when the pain began to subside and more immediate problems occupied my mind, I would turn away and forget about Him again."*—Allen Clark explaining the God apathy that would move in when the pressure was off (page 201, *Wounded Soldier, Healing Warrior*).

As a young infantry lieutenant, Bob Dees also learned that the most dangerous time on the battlefield is after the firing has stopped. As a young platoon leader, I can recall many instances in training and simulated combat when we would take an objective, pop our chests up, and report a great victory to higher headquarters, only to be overwhelmed by an enemy counterattack or dis- cover that we had fallen into a trap. It is called the "consolidation phase" in military tactics, where one reestablishes a strong defense against potential counterattacks, dismantles booby traps and marks unexploded ordnance, treats casualties, processes prisoners of war, resupplies with new rations, water, and ammunition, gathers avail- able intelligence, and makes new plans.

Yet, this is also the very time when troops and leaders are tired, the time when folks tend to let down their guard, not recognizing how vulnerable they are to an enemy counterattack or how much they need to replenish weakened capabilities. Our young infantry sergeant would know this as a time when his soldiers are greatly looking forward to "dry socks on the objective," but one where he as a leader needs to keep their heads in the game and avoid a natural "relaxation response." So it is when one transitions from "weathering the storm" to "bouncing back." We must not relax, for several good reasons.

A first reason for pressing into God is illustrated by the Warrior David, who knew that if he did not have God, he did not have any- thing. When the bottom has fallen out, we must press into God, we must depend, trust, and be consoled as with David in Psalm 18 (underlined emphasis added):

"The Lord is my rock and my fortress and my deliverer, My God, my rock, in whom I take refuge; My shield and the horn of my salvation, my stronghold. (v. 1, 2)

"In my distress I called upon the Lord, and cried to my God for help. He heard my voice out of His temple, and my cry for help before Him came into His ears. (v.6)

"They confronted me in the day of my calamity, but the Lord was my stay. He brought me forth also into a broad place; He rescued me, because He delighted in me. (v. 18, 19)

"The Lord lives, and blessed be my rock; and exalted be the God of my salvation." (v. 46)

And note that David closes with gratitude, "Therefore, I will give thanks to You among the nations, O Lord." (v. 49) We will soon discuss gratitude in greater detail.

A second reason for pressing into God, even harder than when the incoming was crashing around your ears, is that there is never a clear demarcation between the storm and the recovery. As with the premature optimism that comes with the eye of a hurricane, one needs to be wise about the duration of the storms we face. Most trials and tribulations last somewhat longer than we would anticipate or hope for, and we do well to not be surprised or shocked by this persistent nature of trauma.

> Most trials and tribulations last somewhat longer
> than we would anticipate or hope for.

Using another weather analogy, the earthquake "aftershocks" of trauma are real and often severe, sometimes more devastating than the original quake. There will be "triggers" that reignite painful memories—the sights, sounds, smells, interactions with others, normal experiences that act as windows back into a painful past. These triggers often stimulate waves of grief, flashes of anger, despair, and doubt. The journey is like being on a roller coaster: some good days, some painful days, one day at a time and the ride lasts longer than you would think or desire.

For many, such as the thousands of wounded warriors with debilitating injuries, the ride never ends, but God can help us adapt to our "new normal." *New normal* is a term adapted to many uses within the military, all indicating new conditions faced by groups such as military children of deployed parents, families that reintegrate after the military member comes home with trauma, warriors transitioning to civilian life, and other transition scenarios. In these new conditions God helps us live meaningful and joyful lives. While we never forget the loved one who has been taken away from us, the shattered dreams, the radically altered plans, or the loss of who we once were, God can use the pain and suffering to stimulate a *new spiritual normal* that not only allows us to bounce, but to bounce even higher in the Lord than we ever thought possible. This occurs as we "press into God" desperately and passionately, particularly after it seems that the storm has passed, a time when we might be tempted to let up, to relax, to become apathetic.

A third very practical reason for pressing into God is that He is the only true healer. In Exodus 15:25-27, God tells Egypt "...I, the LORD, am your healer." (emphasis added)

On the battlefield when troops are wounded, they don't call for the general; they unashamedly call for the medic and the chaplain to help mend their wounds of the body and soul. Certainly God works through our many great medics, chaplains, physicians, mental health professionals, pastors, counselors, family and friends, but God is the ultimate healer. Psalm 147:3 (parenthesis and under-lines added) reminds us that "He (God) heals the broken hearted and binds up their wounds." As well, Psalm 34:18, 19 (underlines added) reminds us that "The Lord is near to the brokenhearted, and saves those who are crushed in spirit. Many are the afflictions of the righteous, but the Lord delivers him out of them all." We must continue to press into this Healer God as the process of bouncing back extends from days to weeks to months. Failure to do this is a key reason trauma sufferers, including seemingly strong Christians "get stuck" in their recovery.

While there are many strategies, techniques, and tools to recovery from trauma, the ultimate success factor, the "secret sauce," is to never quit pressing into the God who created you, who loves you, who will heal you, and who will continue to use you powerfully in the lives of others.

> The ultimate success factor, the "secret sauce," is to never quit pressing into the God who created you, who loves you, who will heal you, and who will continue to use you powerfully in the lives of others.

<u>The second dimension of Guard Your Primary Relationships deals with the most inner circle of family and friends, our core human relationships</u>. My observation is that organizations and primary relationship groupings (such as family, small group study members, and inner circle associates) often attack inward when faced with an external threat or confusing crisis. Ironically, our closest loved ones sometimes take the full blast of anger, venting, and even violence. It is imperative that we resist this tendency and temptation toward such actions which serve to alienate our closest supporters at the time we need them the most. Conversely, we need to draw close to these supporters, and guard these fundamental relationships.

This begins between husband and wife. Over the years of challenges and body slams, Kathleen and I coined a phrase to apply to such situations: "We are not the enemy." In essence this simple expression, often shared between us during times of trauma and stress, is a simple reminder to "close ranks" and link arms against the perceived threat, whose true identity we discussed in "Know Your Enemy" in Chapter 5. The same principle applies to other close family and inner circle friends; it is critical to intentionally draw close to avoid a wedge in key relationships at such a critical time.

One other observation and caution about close family and friends who "stick closer than a brother." (Proverbs 18:24) There will be times God's Holy Spirit comforts you beyond all measure, when God holds you in the palm of His Hand and personally gives you gratitude and forgiveness as you begin to bounce back. Yet, some of your closest supporters may not have the same capability or desire to graciously respond. They also have been wounded by your trauma, and they are sometimes inclined to strike out in anger or vengeance or frustration or pain on your behalf. In this case, you may find yourself as a voice of reason, one who must counsel forgiveness, gratitude, adopting a patient and reasoned approach, and ultimately love and acceptance towards the perceived source of the woundedness. Your closest supporters may periodically need the Romans 12:17 exhortation: "Never pay back evil for evil to anyone. Respect what is right in the sight of all men." This is certainly the scripturally correct approach, as well as a pragmatic way to avoid further complications when your well-intending friends want to strike out on your behalf.

Choose Forgiveness and Gratitude

We noticed the very attractive and distinguished older couple facing toward us from their table at the small restaurant in Gerrards Cross, England. Kathleen and I were new to town, just having moved to England to attend the Royal College of Defence Studies (RCDS) in London. Anxious to meet new friends and learn more about the "foreign" country in which we would live for the next year, I asked the man if he played squash, a popular British racquet sport. The man replied, "Yes." Thus began a very fulfilling relationship between an American and a British couple, both anxious to learn and enjoy the unique culture of one another.

As we befriended Grant and Caroline (names changed in respect for the family situation), the conversations moved to deeper, more personal topics. One day Caroline asked if we would like to meet her older sister (older by just a year). We met them outside her sister's home and rang the bell. Her sister answered, yet was not in any way distinguishable as Caroline's sister—she looked much, much older; her demeanor was halting, her speech was not the light, vivacious rhetoric we had come to expect from Caroline. Perhaps this radical difference between the close sisters was due to a health issue, or unique trauma, or some other distinctive. Over the course of the evening we learned much more. The two sisters, whose father was a British naval attaché in Hong Kong during the early days of World War II, with their family, had been overrun and interred by the invading Japanese in the Camp Stanley detention camp. As very attractive teenage girls in a Japanese detention camp, their fate was unspeakable.

Note: History records that over 10,000 women and children were raped by Japanese soldiers in the first month of the Japanese takeover of Hong Kong:
(http://www.economist.com/node/1825845?story_id=1825845).
For additional information regarding Japanese brutality toward British women, see website:
http://www.tandfonline.com/doi/pdf/10.1080/09612029600
200119 (pp. 373, 379).

Now, many decades after repatriation and living independently of each other, the sisters resided near one another, yet their lives had turned out quite differently. We soon understood that the only true difference between these two close sisters was the way in which they had responded to similar traumatic circumstances, the way in which one harbored "offense" while the other loosened her grip on the abject violation of her very identity as a person. In the words of our Chapter 3 discussion, one sister had clearly grown bitter and even decades after was "defined" by this traumatic experience of her youth. She had gotten "stuck in the muck," unable to bounce back to a new and fulfilling life. Caroline, on the other hand, had gotten better, she was able to loosen her grip on the painful memories by forgiving her captors and adopting a grateful approach to her circumstances. In her 90's now, she remains a very dignified and gracious lady. She has stood the test of time and the most challenging circumstances that life could throw at her.

When trauma strikes, such as it did for these two young ladies in a Japanese prison camp, one of the first human responses is to get even, to strike back, to take up offense against God or against fellow man. As we see, such offense and its negative consequences can last a lifetime. In *The Bait of Satan*, John Bevere makes profound observations regarding the harboring of offense which leads to long term captivity to bitterness: "The Greek word for "offend" in Luke 17:1 comes from the word *skandalon*. This word originally referred to the part of the trap to which the bait was attached. Hence the word signifies laying a trap in someone's way. In the New Testament it often describes an entrapment used by the enemy. Offense is a tool of the devil to bring people into captivity." (page 7)

One of the temptations we all face when we have been body slammed is to entertain such a Spirit of Offense. Such a mindset certainly disrupts personal peace and collective unity, and it definitely heads us in the wrong direction emotionally and spiritually. Hence, this is a situation, an attitude, a mindset, a spirit we should flee from. This is another primary reason that people get stuck in their grieving and healing process—the harboring of offense which allows roots of bitterness to sink deeply into our emotions and eventually into their very souls. While the degree to which we have been violated personally varies widely across the entire spectrum of trauma, the biblical principles regarding offense and forgiveness remain the same.

John Bevere continues, "By now you see how serious the *sin* of offense is. If it is not dealt with, offense will eventually lead to death. But when you resist the temptation to be offended, God brings great victory." (page 21) In short, we may not be able to control the pain and suffering which invade our lives, but we through Christ can control our response, we can resist this bait of Satan.

> One of the temptations we all face when we have been body
> slammed is to entertain such a Spirit of Offense.

How do we do this? I call it, "Fleeing the Spirit of Offense." Why *fleeing*? My mind turns to the story of Joseph who was trapped and tempted by Potiphar's wife. (Genesis 39) It was not enough to politely say "No" nor was it sufficient to simply walk away. He had to flee, even without his garments, to break the enticement of that temptation. Or consider a counterexample, the story of Lot's wife in Genesis 19:26. While escaping from the doom and destruction of Sodom & Gomorrah, she disobediently quit fleeing and looked back resulting in eternal condemnation as a pillar of salt. The lesson is clear: we must actively, aggressively, with all our might, flee a spirit of offense that seeks to disrupt our healing process and our fellowship with God and our fellow man.

What are some specific ways to proactively avoid a Spirit of Offense? Recognize that **this is war**. Satan prowls, seeking to devour; offense and bitterness are two of his primary tools. As discussed in Chapter 5, the Armor of God (Ephesians 6) provides essential protection. Additionally, a military maxim says, "The first report is always wrong." Hence, don't jump to conclusions. Develop heightened sensitivity to negative input about others; don't just accept at face value. Assume the best about a fellow human being, grant a gracious benefit of the doubt until facts determine otherwise. Don't entertain or overly empathize with grievances expressed by another that should rightly be discussed in supervisory channels. Resolve interpersonal issues scripturally—one-on-one—then include an associate, then formally within the church or the organization. Exercise accountability regarding rumors and gossip; deal in facts, not fiction. Work hard to keep oneself in check, and lovingly remind others as appropriate. In the words of James 1:19, "everyone must be quick to hear, slow to speak and slow to anger." Trauma and suffering do not give us license to be angry at God, the world, or others. The resulting roots of offense and bitterness will exact too high a price from us and those around us. We must flee the spirit of offense at all cost.

Moving from a spirit of offense to a *spirit of forgiveness* let us consider John Bevere's description (page 126) of Matthew 18, where Jesus instructs us regarding forgiveness:

> "Peter asked, 'Lord, how often shall my brother sin against me, and I forgive him? Up to seven times?' (Matt 18:21, NKJV). He thought he was being generous.

> "But he received a shocking reply. Jesus blew away what Peter considered generous: 'I do not say to you, up to seven times, but up to seventy times seven.' (Matt 18: 21, 22 NKJV).

> "In other words, forgive as God does, without limits."

Such forgiveness of God or others is seldom easy or instantaneous. As an act of obedience, we must speak it, pray it, and eventually we will feel it though it may take days, weeks, and often years. Christ modeled this for us when at the height of betrayal, torture, and a painful death on the Cross, He prayed, "Father, forgive them; for they do not know what they are doing." (Luke 23:34)

Consider the story of Louie Zamperini once again. Wracked in his postwar life by Post-Traumatic Stress Syndrome, alcoholism, and relational dysfunction with his closest loved ones, Louis came to faith in Jesus through the Billy Graham Crusade in Los Angeles in 1949. He was liberated through his new understanding of God's love and forgiveness for him, Louie Zamperini. The night of his commitment to Christ, he immediately poured his alcohol down the drain, trashed his cigarettes, and threw away his secret pornography. "In the morning, he woke feeling cleansed. For the first time in five years, the Bird (his Japanese tormentor in prison camp) hadn't come into his dreams. The Bird would never come again." Finding his dusty Bible, he went to a local park to read and sensed 'profound peace.' "In a single, silent moment, his rage, his fear, his humiliation and helplessness, had fallen away. That morning, he believed, he was a new creation. Softly, he wept." (Account of Louie Zamperini conversion and immediate life transformation, *Unbroken*, pages 387, 388; underline emphasis added)

Yet, there was one final sticking point that Louis Zamperini had to deal with: forgiveness. As with many Vietnam veterans after him, he knew he must return to the site of his worst experiences. A year after his conversion, he wanted to see if his newfound faith would stand the test of facing his captors. "If he should ever see them again, would the peace that he had found prove resilient?" Louie soon had his answer. "In Sugamo Prison (Japan), as he was told of Watanabe's ("The Bird") fate, all Louie saw was a lost person, a life now beyond redemption. He felt something that he had never felt for his captor before. With a shiver of amazement, he realized that it was compassion. At that moment, something shifted sweetly inside him. It was <u>forgiveness,</u> beautiful and effortless and complete. For Louie Zamperini, the war was over." (Account of forgiving his Japanese captors, *Unbroken*, page 392, parenthetical comments and underlining added.)

> Forgiveness is absolutely critical to "getting unstuck" and moving on to a joyful future.

Such forgiveness is absolutely critical to "getting unstuck" and moving on to a joyful future. Jesus Christ offers the same liberation, profound peace, and ability to forgive and move on to our troops and veterans of today—past the nightmares, past the debilitating addictions, and past the continuing war in their hearts and minds. For them, too, and for all of us the war can truly be over.

Forgiveness and gratitude go hand in glove, and are essential to resilient recovery from trauma. Nancy Leigh Demoss' twin books, *Choosing Forgiveness* and *Choosing Gratitude* are very encouraging and profound illuminations of God's heart on these subjects. I strongly recommend them, particularly for those in the "bounce back" phase.

Nancy makes some powerful statements in her Introduction to *Choosing Gratitude* (pages 15-19). I have added the emphasis:

"He (the Lord) has shown me *how vital it is to train my heart* to respond to all of life with *a thankful spirit*, even in situations and seasons that I find unpleasant or difficult."

"I've seen that if I am not *ceaselessly vigilant about rejecting ingratitude and choosing gratitude*, I all-too-easily get sucked into the undertow of life in a fallen world. I start focusing on what I don't have that I want, or what I want that I don't have. My life starts to feel hard, wearisome, and overwhelming."

"I've discovered that *gratitude truly is my life preserver*. Even in the most turbulent waters, *choosing* gratitude rescues me from myself and my runaway emotions. It *buoys me on the grace of God* and keeps me from drowning in what other- wise would be my natural bent toward doubt, negativity, discouragement, and anxiety."

"*It's a choice* that requires constantly *renewing my mind* with the truth of God's Word, *setting my heart* to savor God and His gifts, and *disciplining my tongue* to speak words that reflect His goodness and grace—until *a grateful spirit becomes my reflexive response* to all of life."

"To a significant degree, your *emotional, mental, physical, and spiritual well-being, as well as the health and stability of your relationships with others, will be determined by your gratitude quotient. Cultivating a thankful heart is a safe-guard against becoming bitter, prickly, and sour."*

Nancy's wisdom regarding forgiveness and gratitude is "on target." Ephesians 4:32 exhorts us (emphasis added), "Be kind to one another, tender-hearted, *forgiving each other, just as God in Christ has also forgiven you*." As well, the words of I Thessalonians 5:16-18 remind us "Rejoice always; pray without ceasing; *in everything give thanks*; for this is God's will for you in Christ Jesus." This is the way to bounce. This is the way of truly resilient warriors.

Grieve Well

Grief and mourning are a normal part of The Resilience Life Cycle©, often present in varying degrees in each phase of Before, During, and After. In the words of Jesus in the Sermon on the Mount, "Blessed are those who mourn, for they shall be comforted." (Matthew 5:4) In the words of Dr. Sharon Hart May in *Caring for People God's Way,* page 364, "The grieving process is a natural, innate, God-given means for humans to accept, adjust to, and live on in light of the death of loved ones." The same holds true for other types of losses as well—the loss of a dream, the loss of livelihood, the loss of physical or mental capacity, and ultimately the loss of who we once were, or could have been.

Dr. Hart continues on pages 366 and 372, "Visualize the grieving process, not as linear stages to grow through, but rather as layers of an onion unfolding, or as a spiral, or roller-coaster. Few experience the process in the linear way presented here (referring to the Kubler-Ross five stages of grief: denial, anger, bargaining, depression, and acceptance). (Author note: for more information on Kubler-Ross stages of grief, see http://www.ekrfoundation.org/.)

"Many will report living one or more stages at the same time, or rolling through parts of the process again and again... The entire grief process normally takes from 1 to 3 years to resolve, and must be respected as part of living... For some, the mourning process is delayed or it gets stuck, so the process is revisited numerous times over many years. Furthermore (emphasis added), *just having time pass does not necessarily heal the soul*. It is what a person chooses to do during their healing time that determines the new meaning life takes on."

From these foundations, we can make a few observations about what it means to grieve well. Starting with the last assertion from Dr. Hart, "It is what a person chooses to do during their healing time that determines the new meaning life takes on." In essence, that is a primary focus of this entire book: identifying positive, biblically-based, proactive, and reactive steps toward trauma that lead to new meaning and positive contribution as one bounces back.

As we grieve, a <u>first key step is to invite others into our grieving process</u>, starting with God. We are wise to *invite God into our grief process* because: "The Lord is near to the brokenhearted and saves those who are crushed in spirit." (Psalm 34:18)

As well as inviting God, *inviting others into our grief process* brings about a connectedness and sense of community that are helpful and healthy. In terms of relational fitness, this is where the practice of "having friends and being a friend" pays significant dividends. Deep personal relationships are certainly rewarding when fair winds are blowing, but having trusted family and friends who can walk the painful path of recovery with you is essential.

A second observation is that *grief is a reality that cannot be avoided, yet it is different for everyone*. Those who seek to stuff their emotions and rush past the trauma risk a far broader emotional and spiritual impact that will necessarily have to be dealt with in future months or years. In Dr. Hart's words on page 373, "Stifling emotions does not help the mourning process. Yet, not everyone will express emotions the same way. Respect the quiet, gentle grievers. It is more so those who long to give their grief a bolder voice but for some reason can't—who potentially complicate their mourning process."

Thirdly, recognize that *the grief process takes time*. While the difficult mourning stage normally lasts for a few years, the painful memories last for a lifetime, often resurrected by environmental or relational triggers, remembrance ceremonies, significant dates, or similar trauma in the future. While the nation observed recent 10th Anniversary *historical* commemorations of the terrorist attacks on American soil on September 11, 2001, the family members of the 658 Cantor Fitzgerald employees that died in the North Tower of the World Trade Center will never look at that day as mere "history." Neither will the wives and families of the brave men on Flight 93 who stormed the cockpit of their high jacked airplane look at that day as "history;" rather, the loss of their loved one will always be a very present life experience.

And so it is with each of us—you never forget the knock on the door when you were informed that your soldier died, you never forget seeing your spouse waste away to cancer, you never forget burying a child. For wounded warriors and other sufferers of physical and mental trauma, you never forget the loss of who you once were, or could have been. While these painful memories may dull over time, we as humans never truly forget such loss, or even successfully compartmentalize it to the silent shelves of history.

The process of grieving is not about forgetting; it is about processing the loss over time through the lens of our most deeply held spiritual values. It is about gaining new perspective that leads to strength, hope, and eventually, joy. This is exactly what Jesus was talking about when he prepared his disciples for the trauma they would soon witness at His crucifixion (emphasis added): "Truly, truly, I say to you, that you will weep and lament, but the world will rejoice; you will grieve, but *your grief will be turned into joy*." (John 16:20)

The process of grieving is not about forgetting.

While "grieving well" is different for all of us, let me recommend an excellent resource that presents practical starting points for working through the grief process. On the compact disc, *An Invitation to Comfort: A Healing Journey Through Grief*, Dr. Tim Clinton, President of the American Association of Christian Counselors and author of numerous books, artfully and sensitively leads the sufferer through Accepting, Connecting, Understanding,

Surrendering through Christ, and Continuing to Hope. There are many trauma sufferers who have listened to these comforting messages tens of times, drawing new strength, perspective, and hope from each encounter with this comforting reminder of scriptural principles intertwined with powerful musical selections. This one is definitely in my audio player, ready for the next "body slam" of life or opportunity to help another on their painful path. (http//www. aacc.net/shop)

A final note as we end this chapter: Grief and mourning are very real, and they are normal. Actually grief and mourning are God-given mechanisms to heal our frail bodies, minds, and souls. Although family, friends, doctors, pastors, and other caregivers play a role, God is the only healer. God truly is near to the brokenhearted, and He does save those who are crushed in spirit. An abiding, personal relationship with this God of compassion through the person of Jesus Christ is transformational. That relationship allows us to process our grief and mourning differently. Through Jesus and the indwelling presence of the Holy Spirit Comforter, God truly can and does turn our grief, our mourning, into joy ("you will grieve, but *your grief will be turned into joy*." (John 16:20, underline emphasis added). We also know from Nehemiah 8:10 (underline emphasis added) that this joy becomes our strength: ("Do not be grieved, for the joy of the LORD is your strength.") To complete the cycle, this strength allows us to serve ("Blessed be the God and Father of our Lord Jesus Christ, the Father of mercies and God of all comfort, who comforts us in all our affliction so that we will be able to comfort those who are in any affliction with the comfort with which we ourselves are comforted by God." 2 Corinthians 1:3, 4; (underline emphasis added).

MOURNING to JOY to STRENGTH to SERVICE. This is what "right looks like."

It will take time, but we don't have to get stuck.

We can bounce back, and we can bounce back even higher.

See the *Resilience God Style Study Guide* "AFTER" section to develop personal applications for the principles contained in this chapter.

BOUNCE BUILDERS:

1. Coy, Colonel Jimmie Dean. *Valor: A Gathering of Eagles.* Mobile, AL: Evergreen, 2003.
2. Maranatha! Music. *An Invitation to Comfort: A Healing Journey Through Grief.* Narrated by Dr. Tim Clinton. Nashville: Maranatha! Music, 2008. CD.
   Note: this is a tremendous asset for those in grief. A must for your playlist.
3. *Secretariat.* Directed by Randall Wallace. 2010. Burbank, CA: Walt Disney Studios Home Entertainment. DVD.
4. Acapella. "Be Ye Glad," as recorded in *Acapella Project Volume 1.* Nashville: Benson Records, 2004.
5. Tenth Avenue North. "Healing Begins," as recorded in *the Light Meets The Dark.* Nashville, Reunion Records, 2010.

6. Cronin, Helene. "Lucky Me," http://www.cdbaby.com/cd/ helenecronin.
7. Knopf, Bonnie. "Mend This Broken Heart," contained in *Close To His Heart.* Portland, OR: Free Rain Records, 1994.

ADDITIONAL STUDY:

1. Bevere, John. *The Bait of Satan.* 10th Anniversary Ed. Lake Mary, FL: Charisma House, 2004.
2. Clark, Allen. *Wounded Soldier, Healing Warrior: A Personal Story of a Vietnam Veteran Who Lost His Legs but Found His Soul.* St. Paul, MN: Zenith, 2007.
3. Clinton, Tim, Archibald Hart and George Ohlschlager, eds. *Caring for People God's Way: Personal and Emotional Issues, Addictions, Grief and Trauma.* Nashville: Thomas Nelson/Nelson Reference & Electronic, 2005.
4. DeMoss, Nancy Leigh. *Choosing Forgiveness: Your Journey to Freedom.* Chicago: Moody, 2006.
5. DeMoss, Nancy Leigh. *Choosing Gratitude: Your Journey to Joy.* Chicago: Moody, 2009.
6. Downer, Phil. *From Hell to Eternity: Life After Trauma.* Signal Mountain, TN: Eternal Impact, 2010.
7. Manion, Jeff. *The Land Between: Finding God in Difficult Times.* Grand Rapids: Zondervan, 2010.

8

Bouncing Ahead...
Into a Hopeful Future!

"Okay, Sir. Here is the book for our next briefing," said the sharp young Naval officer who was acting as my executive officer for a typically crazy day in the Spring of 1996 as the "Vice J7" (Operational Plans and Interoperability Directorate for the Joint Staff). Pretty straightforward, I thought, as we sprinted across the Pentagon to our next meeting. While rushing through throngs of Pentagon staffers and the occasional cluster of tourists huddled around their uniformed tour guide, I read, quickly compartmenting the last briefing and bringing new talking points to front of mind for an entirely different topic. This is a skill that senior military leaders and all corporate executives know well. Apparently from the briefing book (which provided meeting details, attendees, talking points, and background information), this next session was with a group of Colonel-level planners from the U.S. Southern Command—military leaders responsible for the regional engagement plan for the whole continent of South America and the Caribbean basin.

Some have said you can walk between any two points in the Pentagon in ten minutes; maybe if you are an Olympic sprinter, that is. We slid into the meeting in the nick of time and immediately I am introduced, front and center on a small stage overlooking a group of thirty astute military professionals who have traveled thousands of miles for an important week of planning. As I look across the audience just before providing my introductory comments, I see a good friend. Something was not right; I knew this friend to be assigned to the U.S. European Command in Stuttgart, Germany; a totally different region of the world! And then another familiar face, also from Europe. *I had been reading from the wrong briefing book!* I quickly did a mid-air mental pivot and welcomed these folks from Europe, emphasizing the relevance of their area of the world.

That was close! I almost missed the mark badly and confused a lot of good people in the process. I'm sure that never happens to you.

In a scene reminiscent of that Pentagon close call, Kathleen and I in February 2009 found ourselves at Fort Bliss, Texas, visiting in the Hope Chapel with Command Chaplain, Colonel Ron Huggler and his very talented wife Sue, a retired Colonel and former Army nurse, herself. Not having truly focused on the specific troop deployment status of Fort Bliss units, I was geared to provide my normal orientation about the wounds of war and the challenges faced by our military society. I was going to attempt to "encourage the troops" in every way possible.

As I looked over the audience before beginning to speak, a déjà vu moment occurred. Where were the men? I found myself in front of a congregation of largely military wives whose husbands were deployed and no doubt a few husbands with deployed wives. I had again been "reading from the wrong book." Like a bright flash of lightning, I recognized that these waiting spouses did not need to hear a single word about the challenges of the military—they were already living them. These folks needed to know that God had "a hope and a future" for each one of them. They did not need to be reminded of their fears and very real pain in many cases; they needed to look up to the living God who could and would give them hope. It was my job to point them in that direction. Once again, I had almost missed the mark, and badly.

As we continue our discussion of "Bouncing Back," it is of uppermost importance for us to not miss the mark as we contemplate and envision the hopeful future that God has planned for each us. No doubt we could all have a pretty good "pity party," but let's spend some time on the other side of the ledger. Specifically, we will learn to move forward and upward to:

- Sing a New Song
- Revalidate Your Calling (Discern and Chart the Future)
- Comfort Others

Sing a New Song

In the introduction to *Mid-Course Correction*, Gordon MacDonald (pages ix, x) discusses a characteristic called "vital optimism" which at its very heart is simply *hope*. MacDonald highlights John Keegan's *The First World War* sobering discussing of the British battle of the Somme, including a statement that this battle was a turning point in British culture, "an age of vital optimism in British life that has never been recovered." While history students might disagree with this assertion (given England's amazing fortitude and resilience in the subsequent World War II), the concept is valid. MacDonald defines this vital optimism as "a quality of spirit possessed by a community or a person where there is a persuasion that the best is yet to be... From such a spirit come increasing excitement, incentive, and the love of nobler purposes." He further states that vital optimism is really hope— "the confident expectation that history is going somewhere and that God, our Creator and Redeemer, is powerfully directing it."

Conversely, when a nation or an individual have been crushed, defeated, "body slammed," there is often a temporary or permanent loss of optimism and hope. Explaining what this dynamic looks like in the lives of warriors (remember, that's all of us!), he continues, "I have known many people who, after a personal strug- gle of some kind (proportionately similar to Britain's tragedy at the Somme), have lost their vital optimism. A man comes to mind who was suddenly terminated from a high-level job. No one, including him, could have foreseen such a possibility. He was devastated; he never really recovered from the shock. Now, more than a dozen years later, he remains stuck in cynicism and bitterness, and as far as I can see, his life is going nowhere." (MacDonald, page x)

Hence, a critical element in "Bouncing Back" without getting stuck is the recovery of "vital optimism" and the recovery of hope for a brighter future. Part of this process is learning to *sing a new song*, a metaphor I will use for the broader concept of being renewed in body, mind, soul, spirit, and relationships as we rise from the ashes of brokenness.

Although not musically gifted, I periodically try to sing—in the shower, in the car, usually away from human ears unless I am really with a trusted friend. When singing a *new* song, my notes are halting, often discordant, exploratory. Yet soon these tentative, plaintiff attempts at melody quickly become robust, clear (at least in my tone deaf ears), and sung to the top of my lungs. Often by surprise, I suddenly find myself singing with total abandon, "going for it," confident and optimistic beyond all expectation.

Similarly, as we obediently seek to sing a new song in our recovery from trauma, we will soon find that the Creator God starts refilling us—putting spring back into our tired steps, igniting sparks of creativity and vision into our depleted minds and hearts, and supernaturally infusing greater clarity and confidence into our dispirited souls.

Have you ever thought much about the power and exhilaration of *new?* Perhaps for you it is the new of gifts on Christmas morning, or maybe the smell of a new car, or the newness and adventure of the first day of a new school year, or a new prosthesis, or starting a new job, or a new baby. With *new* comes expectation, freshness, optimism, and ultimately hope.

Stimulated by a Sarah Young New Year's devotion in *Jesus Calling* for January 1, which stated, "A close walk with God is a life of continual newness...," Kathleen and I did a biblical topic study on *new* with dear friends we were visiting. We were reminded of the many aspects of newness which God has waiting for all of us in the New Year and every day: God is doing a *new thing* among us (Isaiah 43:19), we are *new creations* in Christ... "the old has passed away, and *the new has come*" (2 Corinthians 5:17), we are challenged to put *new wine into new wineskins* (Mark 2:22), Christ is a *new and living way* (Hebrews 10:20), Christ makes *all things new* (Revelation 21:5), Christ gives us a *new commandment* of love (John 13:34), God gives us *new names* to move us into *new realities* (Isaiah 62:2), *His mercies are new every morning* (Lamentations 3:22,23), God transforms our lives through *renewal of our minds* (Romans 12:2), we are challenged to put on the *new man* (Colossians 3:10), and many references to God's Holy Spirit Who sends *new breezes, new comfort* into our lives on a daily basis.

Particularly when you have been body slammed and life as you knew it may have come to an abrupt halt, such reminders of new beginnings are very encouraging, serving to spark optimism, and hope, and dreams for the future. "For I know the plans that I have for you," declares the Lord, "plans to prosper you and not to harm you, *plans to give you hope and a future*." (Jeremiah 29:11, NIV, emphasis added) This awareness that God the Creator is the author of new beginnings, and that He seeks a prosperous and hopeful future for you, is often the spark that helps you start looking forward and not back, that helps you start to *sing a new song.*

Particularly when you have been body slammed and life as you knew it may have come to an abrupt halt, such reminders of new beginnings are very encouraging, serving to spark optimism, and hope, and dreams for the future.

Speaking of singing, have you ever heard of anyone singing in prison? From the Book of Acts, we learn about some really "crazy dudes" named Paul and Silas. The head dude, the Apostle Paul actually, had chosen a faithful man, Silas, as his "battle buddy" on his missionary journey into Macedonia. Early in the journey in the vicinity Philippi they had great success in spreading the hope of Jesus to the Gentile people, but they soon encountered opposition. In fact, they got "body slammed" pretty bad. They were falsely accused by some local businessmen, convicted by a "kangaroo jury," reviled by a rioting mob, beaten with rods, and thrown into prison with their feet in stocks. Now, that's pretty tough stuff. Maybe you have been through similar circumstances. For many of us, that would be the "egg splat," game over!

Yet, this was not Paul and Silas' first rodeo. They had learned to be content, to be resilient, and to bounce back in all circumstances. "...for I have learned to be content *in whatever circumstances* I am. I know how to get along with humble means, and I also know how to live in prosperity; in any and every circumstance I have learned the secret of being filled and going hungry, both of having abundance and suffering need. I can do all things through Him who strengthens me." (Philippians 4:11-13, emphasis added)

I'm sure one of the keys to such resilience was their ability to *sing a new song*, and we have a prime example: "But about midnight Paul and Silas were <u>praying and singing hymns of praise</u> to God, and the prisoners were listening to them..." (Acts 16:25, emphasis added). I'll leave it to you to read the remainder of the amazing account of the ensuing earthquake and the salvation of the jailer who was charged with insuring their captivity, but let's not miss the point regarding resilience. I don't think they were praying and singing because they were comfortable or just because they were such godly men; I think they had developed the mental and spiritual reflex to look up, not down; forward, not back. Praying and singing a new song (even in prison!) was a means to stand firm and courageous, as well as to invoke God's presence, and have a powerful impact in the lives of those listening, especially when despair and discouragement would be the more logical and predictable emotions.

So it is with each of us. If we are to "bounce back and not get stuck," then we must at some point "sing a new song" which may include actual singing, but more importantly new beginnings, new dreams, new life-giving relationships, and new depth of meaning and purpose with the God who created you, loves you, and has good plans for you in the future.

Develop the mental and spiritual reflex to look up, not down; forward, not back!

Revalidate Your Calling (Discern and Chart the Future)

When one seeks to sing a new song, to move beyond "The Land Between" to "The Promised Land" (again alluding to the wanderings of the nation of Israel), it is useful to have a process by which to discern and chart the future. A gentleman in Dallas, Texas jumpstarted my thinking about this when he introduced me to the concept of a "personal board of directors." In essence, for times of decision and transition one creates a small group, consisting of three or four couples, that constitutes your personal board for a predetermined, limited duration. As mentioned previously, when one is rebounding, they are particularly vulnerable to making premature or unwise life decisions. Hence, making yourself and your spouse open and accountable to this small "board" of friends is extremely valuable.

During those long days in the Pentagon working on the Army Staff and the Joint Staff, I became familiar with a process called "Zero Based Budgeting," a technique where one wipes the slate clean, and identifies requirements, costs, and priorities "from the ground up." Similarly, a useful tool to assist you and your personal board is to create a "personal life budget" from the ground up. This is not a "dollars and cents" budget to examine financial expenses and revenues; rather, it is a budget that shapes the allocation of personal time, passions, energies, relational investments, and professional endeavors.

Starting with a clean slate, look at the "fixed costs" of one's life, the "must do's," the true priorities. This piece represents a golden opportunity to reestablish healthy, biblical life patterns that stand the test of time, escaping unhealthy or unproductive ruts that you may have fallen into over time. It's sort of like an "extreme makeover."

> Start with a clean slate, look at the "fixed costs" of one's life, the "must do's," the true priorities.

There are no doubt a number of ways to categorize our "fixed costs," but for my purposes "The Great Commandment" works well as a biblical template for the key priorities in our lives. From Mark 12:28-31 (parenthesis and underlining added):

> "One of the scribes came and heard them arguing, and recognizing that He (Jesus) had answered them well, asked Him 'What commandment is the foremost of all?' Jesus answered, 'the foremost is, HEAR O ISRAEL! THE LORD OUR GOD IS ONE LORD; AND YOU SHALL LOVE THE LORD YOUR GOD WITH ALL YOUR HEART, AND WITH ALL YOUR SOUL, AND WITH ALL YOUR MIND, AND WITH ALL YOUR STRENGTH. The second is this, YOU SHALL LOVE YOUR NEIGHBOR AS YOURSELF. There is no other commandment greater than these.'"

This is an ideal way to view something we will call Comprehensive Personal Fitness (CPF), the balanced and prioritized integration of the emotional (heart), spiritual (soul), mental (mind), physical (strength), and relational (your "neighbor," starting with family and friends) aspects of your life.

Under each of these categories—physical, mental, spiritual, emotional, relational—you list objectives. For example:

- *Physical* would be health and fitness objectives, along with workout frequencies that consume time and energy.
- *Mental* would include an objective to read one book a month, take college courses, study online, etc.
- *Spiritual* may involve daily devotions, honoring the Sabbath, and participation in a weekly small group.
- *Emotional* may involve practices to maintain a balanced and a positive outlook, avoiding depression and despair.
- *Relational* would activities that enhance relational health, such as participating in a small study group with others, recreation together with a best friend, and healthy family practices.

From a personal life budgeting perspective, a realistic assessment of the time and energies these objectives will be extremely valuable. When you capture these Comprehensive Personal Fitness (CPF) factors across all the categories of first importance in your life, you form a "Values Map." The map depicts your most basic core values that you seek to live out as well as the realities of time, focus, and energy to actually do it. This exercise is also an important reminder that there is a very real cost to such a grounded and balanced lifestyle, but that the rewards are incalculable particularly for one who is bouncing back or in a major life transition.

> This exercise is also an important reminder that there is a very real cost to such a grounded and balanced lifestyle, but that the rewards are incalculable particularly for one who is bouncing back or in a major life transition.

Laying out this Values Map with your personal board of directors is a tangible way to "put your money where your mouth is," to operationalize Jesus' exhortation in the Sermon on the Mount, to establish clear priorities and live them out: "But seek first His kingdom and His righteousness, and all these things will be added to you." (Matthew 6:33)

Next, look at the "variable costs" in your personal life budget. With the remaining time left in one's year, including the time devoted to rest, one then budgets the variable costs. These are decisions over which we have full control, consisting of the discretionary allocation of remaining time, passion, and energies across personal and professional domains. Time is a precious commodity; you will have to make tough decisions about how to use this non- renewable resource. After reserving time for your value priorities, your professional options, which greatly depend upon your stage in life, will now compete across roughly 2000 hours or less in a full year, assuming five eight-hour work days, five days a week, for fifty weeks of the year. I encourage you not to scoff at what may seem to be a small number devoted to your professional life. Although your particular role in the military or in business may exact far more of you "for a season," you will quickly deplete your "well of courage" if you constantly "burn the candle at both ends," you will run out of "margin" as Eric Swenson so aptly addresses in his book, *Margins*. The second book in the Resilience Trilogy, *Resilient Leaders*, addresses self-care and refilling our well of courage in far greater detail.

The basic questions now become how to spend these remaining hours, and how to draw boundaries and expectations in the family, the community, and workplace. This will take the form of a "Mission Map" which includes key areas of endeavor.

For Kathleen and me, the Mission Map involves categories such as speaking, writing, consulting, and advising in our ministry to troops and their families. These areas will be different for each person and couple, reflecting different gifts, skills, life experiences, and passions.

Under the categories, one lists the options under consideration. For example under consulting, I might consider: "Devote 25% of my professional time to consulting for Company X." There goes 500 hours! Do I really want to do that? Can I afford it, in terms of time? Across all categories, you will clearly find far "more Hooah than Dooah" as our wise infantry sergeant would say, meaning we have abundant enthusiasm for many activities but lack the ability to truly do them, at least do them well within the context of a balanced lifestyle. All potential outside commitments translate into allocations of time, passion, keyed to your gifts, talents, and life goals; and energy, keyed to your physical stamina and demands upon your physical and mental energies.

The overall objective of this personal and professional budgeting drill is obviously to deal with the reality of limited time and limited capacity. Obtaining wisdom from the personal board of di- rectors is particularly valuable during this stage. Assuming you are sufficiently open and vulnerable, they will provide the invaluable "wisdom of many counselors" (Proverbs 15:22) as they help you be sufficiently introspective regarding the why and how of the future life options you are considering.

Although the Values Map and the Mission Map are very process oriented, they help one move from subjective to objective consideration of options and greatly assist you and your personal board in separating wheat from chaff, in making wise decisions regarding competing alternatives. Over time they will provide a useful touch- stone for "periodic maintenance checks" of your life balance.

As a last piece of wisdom on this subject of "Discern and Chart the Future," a highly respected friend in Dallas, Texas, provided another simple nugget: "Practice your declinations." In short, he was saying that transition brings new opportunities, many of which you should say "No" to. The term *practice* implies that one should learn to say "No" well, graciously, not burning bridges, leaving the door open to future engagements when the time is more opportune. As mentioned in "Sing a New Song," the transition which usually accompanies pain and trauma is often a "cleverly disguised opportunity" to build new margin in one's life and regain balance. This includes having a healthy willingness to say "No" graciously.

Comfort Others

"How will we recognize you?" Kathleen asked, to determine how we would meet a new friend at a crowded women's conference in a Dallas hotel. Lacie Habekott, soon to graduate from Dallas Theological Seminary and enter into ministry to military men and women at the U.S. Air Force Academy, simply responded, "Well, I'm not sure what I will be wearing, but I do walk with a limp." Later in the day, we met Lacie for the first time. Approaching from a distance, she was a strikingly beautiful, statuesque young woman with an exceedingly joyful countenance. And, yes, she did limp a bit... on her one leg.

While blossoming into a very gifted athlete, this unassuming and wonderfully wholesome Oklahoma teenager experienced a tragic auto accident at age 15, not only ripping away her right leg, but also her hopes and dreams for the future—at least momentarily. This innocent young teen did not "deserve" this, yet, as with so many others we have written about in these pages, her faith, family, and friends allowed her to weather this tragic blow, to bounce back even higher than before, to accomplish wonderful life goals, and to speak with a unique credibility into the lives of others, particularly those who may have suffered similar tragedy.

In the words of scripture, Lacie became a living epitome of the words in 2 Corinthians 1:3, 4 (emphasis added): "Blessed be the God and Father of our Lord Jesus Christ, the Father of mercies and God of all comfort, *who comforts us in all our affliction so that we will be able to comfort those who are in any affliction* with the comfort with which we ourselves are comforted by God."

Not only does God love us and comfort us, He also has higher purposes for our suffering *so that* we may comfort others. As we do this, God accelerates our own healing process, largely because our focus turns from our own travails to the rewarding opportunity to help others. God truly does give us a unique "voice" into the lives of others when we encourage them through His strength because we have walked down their paths.

No doubt you have seen this in action. For example, combat veterans often open up best with other combat veterans, often defying normal generational barriers; young and old warriors together sharing a common identity and drawing strength from one another. When I introduce our family picture to a group of business professionals, or military wives, or young marrieds, and mention, "And Kathleen and I have a third child, our daughter Amy, who is waiting for us in heaven," those who have lost a child of their own resonate with our story. This has happened many times since 1975 when we lost our first child, Amy, at birth.

Just recently a middle-aged mother, also a very accomplished Navy retiree, approached us in tears after an event. She related that she had lost two children at young ages, and was willing to be vulnerable with someone who perhaps had experienced the same heartache. When we walk with a limp; we are often able to uniquely comfort others.

And so it is: Vietnam Veterans Allen Clark and Phil Downer, Gold Star Parents Susan and Deacon Collins, Iraq Wounded Warrior Scotty Smiley and his amazing caregiver wife Tiffany, the resilient and joyful victim of a drunk driver Lacie Habekott, and so many others have this unique ability to comfort others, largely because they "walk with a limp." And don't we all?

Let's look at this for a moment in terms of stewardship. God taught His people about stewardship from the beginning of creation: stewardship of the Garden of Eden (Genesis 1:26-30, 2:15), stewardship when God asked Moses in Exodus 4:1-5 what he had in his hand. "Throw it down, Moses," God commanded. As Moses released his grip on this simple rod, this inanimate tool became an animate demonstration of God's power and an implement to change the course of a nation. In John 6:8-11 a little boy demonstrated stewardship as he loosened his grip on the loaves and fishes in his hands, releasing them to the multiplying power of Jesus for the benefit of five thousand families and the glory of God. No doubt you could also give many examples.

The principle is this: In life, we find different things in our hands: wealth, influence, access, gifts, and talents. We are called to take what is in our hands, release our grip, and allow God to use our meager offerings to His glory, for the benefit of others.

This applies equally to the "stewardship of pain." As we pry our fingers loose from our violated rights, our broken dreams, our inexplicable tragedies, God takes our life experiences and multiplies them for good in the lives of others. And, we get the joy of being an instrument of healing in the life of another; one of life's "priceless" gifts.

This stewardship of pain, comforting others with that which we have been comforted, is a key to not getting stuck in our healing process. Regrettably, many trauma sufferers remain self-absorbed to the degree that they become professional "victims." Like the Dead Sea in Israel, they continue to take in comfort and help from others but do not allow an outbound flow which releases the same comfort to others in their affliction. The result is stagnation, getting stuck, a veritable dead sea with stagnation of spirit and soul.

> Stewardship of pain, comforting others with that which we have been comforted, is a key to not getting stuck in our healing process.

An important section of scripture in Galatians Chapter 6 has two seemingly contradictory instructions that actually frame this necessary balance between being comforted and comforting others, between dependency on others and service to others. Galatians 6:2 states, "Bear *one another's burdens* and therefore fulfill the law of Christ." Yet Galatians 6:5 says, "For each one must *bear his own load.*" Which is it? Do we bear one another's burdens, or do we carry our own loads? Gratefully, the original Greek wording lends some insight. Apparently the wording for "one another's burdens" is *baros* (an unwieldy and overwhelming burden) while the original language for "our own loads" is *phortion* (referring to a personal knapsack).

Our proverbial infantry sergeant will identify with these passages. No self-respecting infantryman would let someone else carry their personal load, their "rucksack" with essential personal items, unless they were wounded or exhausted, and then for only as short a time as possible. On the other hand, there are some things that take teamwork, such as "crew-served" weapons like a heavy machinegun which is beyond the human capability of most NFL linemen to carry for very long. Hence, someone carries the tripod, someone carries the extra ammunition, and someone or more than one carries the machinegun itself. This burden must be shared.

It is the same in God's economy of comfort. When we have been body slammed, we should not try to carry unrealistic burdens and excessive weights by ourselves. We need help, and there are many around us who are glad to share the burden. We should, however, attempt to "pull our own weight," carry our own rucksack as soon as possible; and to begin to lend a shoulder to the collective team effort for the benefit of others. Otherwise, we "get stuck" in persistent dependency on others with the peripheral downside of co-dependency on the part of our closest caregivers. Comforting others moves us away from any vestige of an unhealthy, lingering victim mentality, and ushers us into new realms as healthy caregivers.

As a final illustration, Kathleen and I were in the burn ward in Brooke Army Medical Center (BAMC). We were now familiar with "suiting up" in the sterile protective garments, head to foot, which would maintain the essential isolation from outside germs that would be life threatening to these critical burn patients. Among the patients we sought to encourage, we were particularly interested in reconnecting with Sergeant Merlin German (burned over 97% of his body by an IED in Iraq), and his dear mother from the Dominican Republic who had been at his bedside continuously for a period of months while his medical condition remained precarious.

Carefully shepherded by the expert and compassionate BAMC medical staff, we entered Merlin's room. After admiring his plastic surgeon's artwork (new ears, eyelids, and other facial parts which had literally been missing when we visited Merlin the first time), we passed along our inadequate but heartfelt words of gratitude and encouragement. Then it was Merlin's turn. Graciously and humbly deflecting any sympathy directed his way, he slowly and painfully asked, "Have you met Sgt (name deleted) yet?" referring to another wounded warrior in an adjacent room. "He hasn't seen his family for some time, and I think he might be lonely." With tears in our eyes, we responded that we would be glad to look in on Merlin's newest battle buddy, for whom he had greater concern than for himself.

We suddenly became the students of giving comfort. Merlin had demonstrated the unselfish nobility that we observe in so many wounded warriors, military and otherwise, who "walk with a limp" from the brutality of war or the battles of life, comforting others with that which they have been comforted.

As a note, Sgt. German succumbed to his battle injuries on April 11, 2008, but his battle for life and his consideration of others left a legacy in the annals of Brooke Army Medical Center and beyond. He personified *Semper Fidelis*, the USMC motto, meaning "Always Faithful." You can learn more by doing an Internet search for "Sergeant Merlin German USMC."

Great job! We have completed the "Bouncing Back" discussion of the Resilience Life Cycle©:

- Guard Your Primary Relationships
- Choose Forgiveness and Gratitude
- Grieve Well
- Sing a New Song
- Discern and Chart the Future
- Comfort Others

Now we move into the final piece of the Resilience Life Cycle©, discussing the feedback loop in "Getting Ready...Again!"

RESILIENCE LIFE CYCLE©

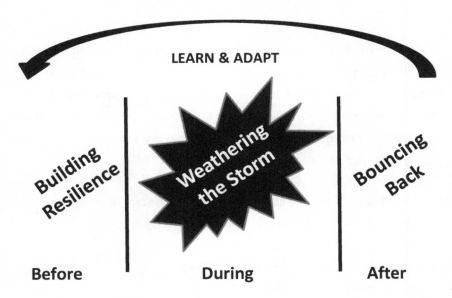

LEARN & ADAPT

Building Resilience

Weathering the Storm

Bouncing Back

Before   **During**   **After**

See the *Resilience God Style Study Guide* "AFTER" section to develop personal applications for the principles contained in this chapter.

BOUNCE BUILDERS:

1. Morgan, Robert J. *Then Sings My Soul: 150 of the World's Greatest Hymn Stories.* Nashville, TN: Thomas Nelson, 2003.
2. *Lean on Me.* Directed by John G. Avildsen. Produced by Norman Twain. Burbank, CA: Warner Bros., 1989. DVD.
3. www.ResilienceGodStyle.com, as well as Twitter (@GodBounce) and FB (Resilience God Style), for supplementary faith-based resilience content and inspiration.

4. Selah. "Press On," as recorded in *Press On.* Nashville: Curb Records, 2001.

5. Phillips, Craig, and Dean. "From The Inside Out," as recorded on *Fearless.* Nashville: Ino/Columbia, 2009.

6. Acappella. "It Is Well With My Soul," as recorded in *Hymns for all the World.* Nashville: Sony, 1994.

7. Knopf, Bonnie. "Place of Rest," as recorded in *Do Not Fear.* Portland, OR: Nuggets of Truth, 2009. http://www.bonnieknopf.com

ADDITIONAL STUDY:

1. Adsit, Chris, Rahnella Adsit and Marshéle Carter Waddell. *When War Comes Home: Christ-Centered Healing for Wives of Combat Veterans.* Newport News, VA: Military Ministry, 2008.

2. MacDonald, Gordon. *Mid-Course Correction: Re-Ordering Your Private World for the Next Part of Your Journey.* Nashville: Thomas Nelson, 2005.

3. Light University. *Stress & Trauma Care: With Military Application.* Forest, VA: Light University, 2009. Counseling Certificate Training Program. DVD series. http://www.lightuniversity.com

4. Light University. *Stress & Trauma Care: With Military Application.* Forest, VA: Light University, 2009. Counseling Certificate Training Program. Workbook. http://www.lightuniversity.com

9

Getting Ready...
Again!

I was turning a little green with the bumpy weather as I flew to the drop zone with fellow 101st Airborne Division jumpers in the back of a Dutch C-130 aircraft. The date was September 17, 1994, exactly 50 years after the 101st's historic jump into Holland as part of Operation Market Garden the largest airborne operation in the history of war. You may remember this from the book and ensuing movie entitled, "A Bridge Too Far," by Cornelius Ryan.

As Brigade Commander of the Rakkasan Brigade in the 101st Airborne Division from Fort Campbell, Kentucky, I was part of a contingent to jump at the 50th Anniversary Commemoration of this operation—same date and time, at the same place, Eindhoven, Holland. The only difference was that 50 years later we would be greeted by cheering and appreciative Dutch citizens, rather than the Nazi occupation force that cunningly waited for the liberating Screaming Eagle paratroopers in September 1944.

"Six minutes!" (Standard Jumpmaster command, shouted over the roar of the engines)

"Get Ready! Outboard personnel stand up! Inboard personnel stand up! Check static lines! Check equipment! Sound off for equipment check!"

"All Okay... All Okay... All Okay, Jumpmaster!" the report ripples from the front of the airplane rearward through the rows of jumpers on both sides of the plane to the waiting Jumpmasters. With the sure knowledge that all jumpers are "hooked up," the jumpmasters (an Assistant Jumpmaster works the other door, assisting the simultaneous exit of the jumpers from both sides of the plane) open the doors, quickly run through safety checks, and lean their upper bodies and heads outside the plane into the rushing wind stream to identify key landmarks on the ground below.

"One minute!" shouts the Jumpmaster as he again thrusts himself out the open door to peer through wind-watered eyes down at the upcoming Eindhoven drop zone.

"Stand in the Door!" commands the Jumpmaster, looking straight into the eyes of the first jumper, grabbing the jumper's static line to avoid the risk of static line malfunction or injury to the jumper. Despite the peaking adrenaline, the Jumpmaster and this first Jumper in the door stand firm, focused, committed, facing fear and danger stoically, conditioned by their training and fortified by the band of fellow warriors watching and waiting for the green light to trigger a rush of sixty-four troopers pushing through the door at one second intervals into the rushing slipstream.

The light flashes from red to green. "Go! Go! Go!"

Thus began my journey on that September day in 1994 above Eindhoven, Holland. Upon exiting the door, I reflexively began the count to four thousand that would be my trigger to activate the reserve parachute, if needed. "One thousand... two thousand... three thousand... Praise the Lord!" I exclaimed as my main chute opened. I quickly pedaled to get the twist out of my risers, shot an eye out for other descending jumpers that might represent a hazard of collision or entanglement and loss of air in my own canopy, and looked downward to gain terrain orientation that would influence any "slips" necessary to land in the right location.

With the roaring aircraft engines now becoming a distant whisper, the silence and the grandeur of the setting were profound. The beautifully green and flat Dutch landscape stretched out below, the epitome of peace and tranquility. As I floated to earth, I recalled those great 101st veterans of 50 years prior—same time, same place—also drifting downward, yet into hostile fire from the Nazis, anticipating that they or many of their battle buddies would not survive the bullets aimed at the vulnerable jumpers, or that they would be quickly captured, wounded, or killed upon landing. These veterans had left everything behind; they were "all in." Most of them had also jumped a few months earlier in Operation Overlord,

Normandy, France, June 1944, jumping behind enemy lines at Utah Beach, enabling a successful breakout from the beaches of Normandy. These were truly brave men, great Americans, and resilient warriors.

I was awakened from my thoughts of respect and reverie as I suddenly remembered the rushing ground below. Now was the time for my training to kick in: feet and knees together, keep those elbows in, good parachute landing fall. Another "Praise the Lord" as my acrobatic airborne landing went smoothly, assisted by the rain-laden Dutch farmland.

While rolling up my parachute to avoid being dragged by wind gusts and to prepare for moving off the drop zone, I was embraced, rather tackled, by an elderly Dutch woman. Crying profusely, she excitedly spoke words in her native tongue that I did not understand. A translator arrived to help the woman tell her story: "The Germans were apprehending and often killing men each day in Eindhoven in those fall months of 1944, trying to keep the Dutch underground in line. My father was apprehended early in the morning. Our family was shattered, traumatized, but what could we do? We were help-less." She then exclaimed with joyful tears, "But then it happened. We saw you, you Screaming Eagles, descending to earth. You saved my father, you saved our land."

Those great Screaming Eagle paratroopers had saved her father, they had liberated Holland from the Nazi grip, and they had begun unhinging the entire continent of Europe from an evil empire. Yet, if you called them "Heroes," they would give the reply you have heard many times: "I was just doing my job, Sir, just doing my job." And so it is with this nation's veterans from Valley Forge forward— they arrive in dark, dangerous places and start putting one boot in front of another, one bloody, dusty combat boot in front of another—saving lives, liberating nations, and unhinging whole continents from evil empires.

This inspiring story honors our veterans and depicts many aspects of the Resilience Life Cycle. In particular, it illustrates the "feedback loop" of the model which describes taking the outcomes of the bounce back phase and feeding them back into the building bounce phase, in anticipation of yet another body slam in future life battles. The reality for these World War II warriors is that they did not have the luxury of fighting just one battle; they had to fight many over the course of four years, and they had to apply every-thing they learned from prior battles to be able to stay alive and succeed in the next.

For many of the 101st Airborne troopers, it meant parachuting behind enemy lines as part of the Normandy D-Day operation (June 6, 1944) to gain a foothold on the continent of Europe, then parachuting again in Operation Market Garden in Holland as the Allies sought open up "Hell's Highway" to flank the Nazis and apply pressure on the German heartland, then tenaciously defending against the surrounding Nazi formations under harsh winter conditions at Bastogne in the Battle of the Bulge, and finally in numerous exploitation efforts, to root out Nazi resistance across the breadth of Europe in places like the Eagles Nest, one of

Hitler's command outposts in the Bavarian Alps of Southern Germany. These warriors fought again, and again, and again.

And so it is with each of us. In each of our respective foxholes of life, we fight, we get wounded, we bounce back, and we fight again, placing one boot in front of the other. As the British philosopher George Santana maintained, "Those who fail to learn the lessons of history are destined to repeat them." So it is in warfare. So it is in life.

The Resilience Life Cycle© aptly illustrates that we must insure we are feeding back to prepare for future life experiences. Notice the feedback loop which you see on the model, below.

RESILIENCE LIFE CYCLE©

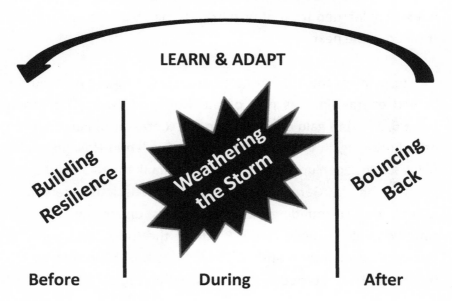

Learn and Adapt

From a more technical perspective, the term *feedback* is defined in *Merriam-Webster's Collegiate® Dictionary* as "the return to the input of a part of the output of a machine, system, or process [to] improve performance or provide self-corrective action." (Used by permission. From *Merriam-Webster's Collegiate® Dictionary* ©2011 by Merriam-Webster, Incorporated, www.Merriam-Webster. com).

The last words in this definition beg the question for each of us: How do we *provide self-corrective action, how do we learn and adapt* our own behaviors and responses to stress and trauma based upon the lessons, the feedback, from previous traumatic experiences?

While there is no prescriptive answer to this, I offer a simple recommendation. Take the areas we highlighted as instrumental in Building Bounce (Chapter 5, *Resilience God Style*) and determine how you might *learn and adapt* within each of these readiness factors as you integrate the lessons learned. Specifically, look at:

- *Know Your Calling.* Has your recent trauma given you new insight on your gifts, your passions, and your sense of God's direction regarding how he can uniquely grow you and use you? With the knowledge that "Threat clears a man's head," you have an advantage: your crisis may have added clarity that further crystallizes your understanding of your destiny and purpose in life. Such clarity often leads to increased focus and commitment to a smaller group of priorities that are truly central to your identity as a person and your capability to serve others.

- *Know Your Enemy*. You have learned new things about yourself. What are the weaknesses and vulnerabilities you should be more aware of in the future? How do you reduce risk in these areas, particularly the three categories listed in 1 John 2:16 (underlining added): "For all that is in the world, the lust of the flesh and the lust of the eyes, and the boastful pride of life, is not from the Father, but is from the world." You have also learned more about others on your traumatic journey. Who can you trust? Who and what must you be cautious about? As well, you have become wiser about spiritual warfare and the Evil One "which wages war against your soul."

- *Know Your Friends*. Some of your "friends" probably headed the other direction when adversity camped on your doorstep, and some friends were "closer than a brother." (Proverbs 18:4) This is useful information for facing the future battles of life. Who do you now trust to cover your back? Who will be a reliable battle buddy in coming days? Who do you want to "grow old with" in friendship and service together? What relationships are "life giving," and what relationships should you not continue or pursue in your next chapters of life? Dr. Jim Dobson, former President and Founder of Focus on the Family, and now Founder and President of Family Talk (http://www.myfamilytalk.com) captures this principle well, "What really matters at the end of life is Who We Loved, Who Loved Us, and What We did in the service of the Lord together." All of these are critical life questions as we learn from the past and invest in life giving relationships for the future.

- *Know Your Equipment.* As you endured trauma and sought to bounce back without getting stuck, what spiritual disciplines were beneficial, which ones broke down under the stress and strain? How do you enhance your spiritual fitness? Did you learn more about the "Armor of God?" How to wear it, use it? What specific parts of the Bible, and other edifying media were especially relevant and restorative to you? How do you make these a part of your own Bounce Builders, and how do you consolidate these in your own life as you begin to comfort and train others?

- *Deploy with the Right Mindset.* Often the awareness of God's provision and comfort, as well as the love and assistance from dear family and friends, increases our gratitude quotient. How do we capture and practice this new found gratitude to God and others in ways that will make this a subconscious reflex? How do we choose forgiveness, recognizing that it is not a one-time event? Note the biblical passage in which Jesus exhorts a forgiving spirit that extends forgiveness to "seventy times seven." (Matthew 18:22) In the context of your personal trauma, this may mean that you don't simply forgive *490* offenses, but that you forgive one offense *490* times. Prayerfully, your trauma has better equipped you to choose gratitude and forgiveness when pressed by future life situations.

- Develop and Rehearse "Actions on Contact." Reflect again on the "Actions on Contact" recommended in Chapter 6, Weathering the Storm. Look at each one with new insight. Capture in your *Resilience God Style Study Guide* the specifics which will pay dividends in the future regarding: Call 911 (crying out to God, Family and Friends, and other caregivers), Start the IV (intensive intake of biblical truth and inspiration), Keep Breathing (continue basic spiritual disciplines despite chaos), Draw from Your Well of Courage (reflect back on prior situations when God provided and comforted), and Remember Your Calling (having clarified your purpose in previous iterations of life trauma so you can remind yourself of your calling when you are knocked to your knees again).

While you are ultimately responsible for capturing your own personal lessons learned in this feedback process, I encourage you to tap the perspective and assistance of close family members and friends, your personal board of directors, and perhaps professional caregivers which might include a life coach, a trusted pastor, or a mental or behavioral health professional. I likewise encourage you to document your trauma "actions on contact" into the *Resilience Battle Book* that is readily available and tailored to your specific use, part of your "important papers" that you safeguard for emergency situations.

Getting It Right: The Story of Joseph

As one more example of this feedback principle, let us reconsider the life of Joseph within the framework of our Biblical Resilience Chapter, 2 Corinthians 4, particularly verses 8 and 9. Joseph's life depicts each of the categories:

- *Afflicted*—he was hated by jealous brothers and sold into slavery (Genesis 37)

- *Perplexed*—he was tempted and falsely accused by Potiphar's wife (Genesis 39)

- *Persecuted*—he was thrown into prison and betrayed by the chief cupbearer (Genesis 40)

- *Struck down*—he spent two or more years in prison (Genesis 41)

Yet, Joseph was never crushed, despairing, forsaken, or destroyed through these challenging life experiences. In fact after these iterations of trauma, he learned and grew in wisdom and strength, maintaining his integrity, and was ultimately appointed by Pharaoh as ruler over all of Egypt. In that role he helped to save the people from drought-induced starvation.

Looking in Joseph's rear view mirror, it is apparent that God truly did have a hope and a future for him. Without such purifying experiences, however, the proud and cocky teenager would never have been fully equipped to be God's man at a moment of great need and opportunity in world history.

What about you? What about me? Will we "fail to learn" the lessons of our own personal history, and will we be condemned to learn them again and again? Or will we be resilient warriors, learning from each difficult life experience, growing better and not bitter, getting stronger with each difficult step, walking into God's highest potential and purpose for our lives, putting one sometimes bloody, often dusty, boot after another, saving lives, liberating nations, and unhinging continents from evil empires?

See the *Resilience God Style Study Guide* "LEARN AND ADAPT" section to develop personal applications for the principles contained in this chapter.

BOUNCE BUILDERS:

1. Rudy. Directed by David Anspaugh. Produced by Robert N. Fried and Cary Woods. Burbank, CA: Columbia Tristar Home Video, 1993.
2. Young, Sarah. *Jesus Calling: Enjoying Peace in His Presence.* Nashville: Thomas Nelson, 2004.
3. Celtic Woman. "You Raise Me Up," as recorded in Celtic Woman. London/New York: Manhattan Records, 2005.
4. Selah. "Press On", as recorded in *Press On*. Nashville: Curb Records, 2001.

5. Maranatha! Praise Band. "If The Lord Had Not Been On Our Side," as recorded on *Praise Band 9 – Forever*. Nashville: Maranatha! Music, 1999.

ADDITIONAL STUDY:

1. Bonhoeffer, Dietrich. *The Cost of Discipleship.* New York: Touchstone, 1995.
2. Stowell, Joseph M. *The Upside of Down: Finding Hope When It Hurts.* Grand Rapids: Discovery House, 2006.
3. Swenson, Richard. *Margin: Restoring Emotional, Physical, Financial, and Time Reserves to Overloaded Lives.* Colorado Springs; NavPress, 2004.

10

And Even Higher

"Oh, my God!" exclaimed the Pilot-in-Command (PIC) of my command ship, a UH-60 Blackhawk helicopter. A sensation of drag on the chopper's airframe was immediately followed by a bright blue flash. The protective wire cutter just below the rotor housing on the Blackhawk had just sliced through a high voltage transmission line near the boundary between Macedonia and Bulgaria. The helicopter started vibrating violently, with loss of essential operating systems shorted out by the huge influx of voltage. We were maybe three hundred feet in the air at the time, above a deep gorge. The Blackhawk began to plummet rapidly with the PIC and his co-pilot in the seat next to him engaged in a life and death struggle to regain control, to achieve autorotation from the powerless blades, to try to coax their steel beast into the best place to land, to save their lives and the lives of eight soldiers ranging from Sergeant to Major General from the V Corps Headquarters operating out of Camp Able Sentry in Skopje, Macedonia.

These pilots did a marvelous job fighting the chaos and control challenges. Through their efforts and some miraculous intervention, the chopper hit a small patch of flat green turf not much bigger than a tennis court. A high road bank loomed above on one side, with a steep creek bed on the other. We hit hard, but our blow was cushioned by last minute autorotation that afforded some lift just before impact.

While everyone was somewhat shaken, no one was killed or seriously injured. Since our mission had been to identify a bypass around Albania guerillas who were threatening the main supply route for United States forces operating as a part of "KFOR" in Kosovo (to the north of Macedonia), we immediately dismounted our door guns and established local security in an uncertain environment, reestablished communications with our Tactical Operations Center (TOC) at Camp Able Sentry in Skopje, Macedonia, and started working next steps.

During this early chaos after the crash, one of the crew chief door gunners came to me totally distraught, ripped the Velcro-attached leather name plate (which also had his Crew Member Badge embossed) from his flight suit, and gave voice to his post-crash trauma: "I can't take any more of this, Sir." Conversely, the other crew chief went about his duties with a far more resilient mindset: an outlook to the crash that I might paraphrase as, "Gee, Sir, that was 'special'— now what's our next mission?" This latter crew chief demonstrated the mindset of today's resilient warriors who, for example, might be heard to repeat familiar Ranger mantras such as, "Pain is just weakness leaving the body," or "What doesn't kill you makes you stronger." Or, from the life of the resilient Apostle Paul in the 2 Corinthians 4 Resilience Chapter: "Therefore *we do not lose heart*, but though our outer man is decaying, yet *our inner man is being renewed* day by day. For *momentary light affliction* is producing for us *an eternal weight of glory* far beyond all comparison, while *we look not at the things which are seen*; for the things which are seen are temporal, but the things which are not seen are eternal." (2 Corinthians 4: 16-18, emphasis added by author)

Although very difficult to ferret out all the factors involved with the contrasting reactions of these two crew chiefs, here again we have two people with similar backgrounds, life experiences, and training who reacted in polar opposite ways. One was clearly more resistant to trauma than the other and more resilient as a person and a warrior. No doubt you have seen the same contrasting reactions to trauma in your world: one person is devastated, while the other is determined, one breaks while the other bounces. For every Allen Clark, Phil Downer, Nate and Julie Self, Robert and Amy Nuttall, Scotty and Tiffany Smiley, Susan and Deacon Collins, and other positive resilience role models we have discussed or that you can name personally, there are many more that did not bounce back, many more that became a statistic, many more that spiraled downward in bitterness, self-medicating addictions, and ultimately life dysfunction, homelessness, hopelessness, and even suicide.

What about You? What about Me?

The question now becomes, "What about you? What about me?" Will we view the inevitable traumas of life through a lens of resilience and potential growth through adversity, or will we be inclined to play the role of a helpless and hopeless victim? The fundamentals of comprehensive fitness, particularly spiritual fitness, which we have discussed in *Resilience God Style* can make the difference, potentially all the difference, for you, me, and everyone else who faces trauma. And who is not in that category?

As a summary of the basics of resilience which we have explained and demonstrated through the life stories of many resilient warriors, note the Resilience Life Cycle© below with the Before, During, and After considerations mapped under each phase:

RESILIENCE LIFE CYCLE©

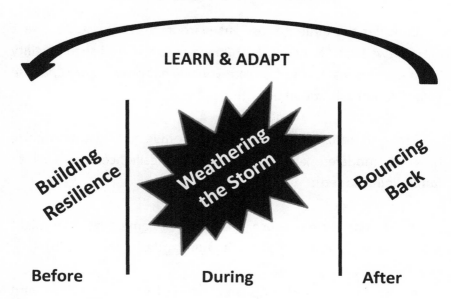

LEARN & ADAPT

Building Resilience

Weathering the Storm

Bouncing Back

Before

During

After

Before
- Know Your Calling (Mission, Purpose)
- Know Your Enemy
- Know Your Friends
- Know Your Equipment (Armor of God)
- Deploy with the Right Mindset
- Develop and Rehearse "Actions on Contact" (Get Ready!)

During
- Call 911 (Ask for help)
- Start the IV (Nurture yourself)
- Keep Breathing (Maintain routines)
- Draw from Your Well of Courage (Past strengths)
- Remember Your Calling

After
- Guard Your Primary Relationships
- Choose Forgiveness and Gratitude
- Grieve Well
- Sing a New Song
- Revalidate Your Calling (Discern and Chart the Future)
- Comfort Others

The Ultimate Resilient Warrior—Jesus Christ

Consider the ultimate resilient warrior, Jesus Christ. As it says in Hebrews 12:3, "For *consider Him* who has endured such hostility by sinners against Himself, *so that you will not grow weary and lose heart.*" (emphasis added by author).

Draw strength and encouragement from Jesus Christ. Recognize how He modeled key aspects of the Resilience Life Cycle© (underlining added):

- He has a clear sense of *calling*: "I came that they might have life and might have it abundantly." (John 10:10b)

- He was invested in his small circle of *friends*: "And He went up on the mountain and summoned those whom He Himself wanted, and they came to Him." (Mark 3:13, 14)

- He was equally *aware* of his large circle of *enemies*: "But the Pharisees went out and conspired against Him, as to how they might destroy Him. But Jesus, aware of this, withdrew from there." (Matthew 12:14,15a)

- He used *God's Word* to *confront* his *enemy*, Satan: for example, "Jesus said to him, "On the other hand, it is written, YOU SHALL NOT PUT THE LORD YOUR GOD TO THE TEST." (Matthew 4:7)

- He observed *disciplines of replenishment*, refilling his well of *courage* and *care giving*: "Now when Jesus heard about John, He <u>withdrew from there in a boat to a secluded place by Himself</u>;" (Matthew 14:13a)

- He comforted others, even at the peak of his torment on the cross. "And He (Jesus) said to him, Truly, I say to you, <u>today you shall be with Me in Paradise</u>." (Luke 23:43)

- He arose again to *sing a new song* and to likewise give us a new song and abundant lives: "Therefore if anyone is   in Christ, he is <u>a new creature</u>; the old things have passed away; behold, <u>new things have come</u>." (II Corinthians 5:17)

When we consider Jesus and draw strength and encouragement from Him, we must also observe His most traumatic moment: the sobering reality when He hung on a cross. Flanked by robbers on each side who were also condemned to death by crucifixion, Jesus remained a role model of resilience, courage, and comfort to others in His darkest hour of physical agony and spiritual separation from His Heavenly Father.

The thieves were both inches away from Jesus; they were experiencing the whole trauma with Him. We can assume again that they also were not too dissimilar in background and life experiences, yet they had totally different reactions to the trauma of physical pain, emotional despair, and impending death. One robber was obstinate and proud, "...hurling abuse at Him, saying, 'Are You not the Christ? Save Yourself and us!'" (Luke 23:39)

The other robber was humble, contrite, and broken. "But the other answered, and rebuking him said, 'Do you not even fear God, since you are under the same sentence of condemnation? And we indeed are suffering justly, for we are receiving what we deserve for our deeds; but this man has done nothing wrong.' And he was saying, 'Jesus remember me when you come in Your Kingdom!' And He said to him, 'Truly I say to you, today you shall be with Me in Paradise.'" (Luke 23:40-43)

Here again we have a stark contrast: one thief on the cross was obstinate and proud, bitter and hopeless. The other thief was humble, contrite, and broken, yet grateful and hopeful. What made the difference? In this case it was *hope*, the hope found in the person of Jesus. This hope is well captured by Max Lucado in his book, *3:16: The Numbers of Hope*. On page 8 of his introductory chapter entitled, "The Most Famous Conversation in the Bible," depicting Jesus' interaction with the inquisitive Pharisee Nicodemus, he defines John 3:16 as the "Hope diamond of the Bible."

"For God

so loved the world

that he gave his one and only Son,

that whoever believes in him

shall not perish, but have

eternal life."

(NIV)

Lucado continues on page 8: "A twenty-six-word parade of hope: beginning with God, ending with life, and urging us to do the same. Brief enough to write on a napkin or memorize in a moment, yet solid enough to weather two thousand years of storms and questions. If you know nothing of the Bible, start here. If you know everything in the Bible, return here. We all need the reminder. The heart of the human problem is the heart of the human. And God's treatment is prescribed in John 3:16.

He loves.

He gave.

We believe.

We live.

The penitent robber on the cross received the ultimate gift of hope, "...Christ in you, the hope of glory." (Colossians 1:27)

So it can be with each of us: a choice, a destiny, a path of retreat, or a journey of resilience, for now and into eternity. One might ask, "What does all this 'God talk' have to do with...

- A wounded warrior with seen or unseen wounds,
- A caregiver who keeps on giving, despite abuse and ingratitude,
- A businessman whose life's work is on the brink of economic extinction,

- A high school educator who feels helpless as young minds slip away into a cultural morass,
- A single homemaker with three children in diapers,
- A new cancer patient navigating the realities of mortality,
- A desperate parent with rebelling teenagers,
- An adult child having to make tough and consequential decisions for an aging parent,
- A spouse whose life's mate has departed this world or left for another affection,
- Any situation in which you feel despair and loss and a deep pain that will not go away?"

The answer is *everything*. The pragmatic truth is that a personal relationship with God through Jesus, a partnership with the indwelling and comforting presence of God's Holy Spirit, and a strong expectation that God does and will provide comfort, wisdom, and strength through the pages of the Bible are incredibly relevant and provide practical means to prepare for trauma, weather its storm, and bounce back without getting stuck, to arrive at an even higher plane of performance and life fulfillment than ever before.

> So it can be with each of us:
> a choice, a destiny,
> a path of retreat, or a journey
> of resilience, for now
> and into eternity.

We are talking about the very essence of spiritual fitness and resilience. I attest to this from my own life as a military warrior, a father, a husband, a businessman, a missionary, and a political leader. In these pages you have also heard the undeniable testimony of many other "expert witnesses."

Faith Makes a Difference

The bottom line is that faith matters. The Christian faith in particular makes a significant difference in success or failure, victory or defeat, and hope or despair in the lives of all warriors in every foxhole of life. There are many important principles and disciplines that factor into physical and mental fitness, and we should definitely embrace these.

Complementary emotional, relational, and spiritual fitness are often more elusive, however. They depend heavily upon the critically relevant element of a vibrant personal faith. I challenge you to likewise embrace the benefits of such a personal faith—before, during, and after trauma—in dealing with ongoing and future body slams of life. You, and those who journey this life with you, will be so glad you did.

> "After you have suffered for a little while, the God of all grace, who called you to His eternal glory in Christ, will Himself perfect, confirm, strengthen, and establish you."
> I Peter 5:10

MY *HOPE* AND *PRAYER* FOR YOU AND ME:

- That you and I will enjoy "Fair weather and following seas" (a traditional U.S Navy benediction),
- But, when the *storms of life* head our way, and they *will,*
- That you and I will be *ready*, having invested in *personal resilience*,
- So when the strong winds blow, you and I will *bend but not break*,
- That we will get *better* and not bitter,
- Become *significant survivors* and not sad statistics,
- Able to *comfort others* with that with which we have been comforted,
- Experiencing *healing, purpose, contribution,* and *joy* beyond what we ever thought possible,
- And in the power of our Creator God that we may:

Bounce Back

Without Getting Stuck

And Even Higher!

See Chapter 10 in the *Resilience God Style Study Guide* to record personal applications from this chapter.

BOUNCE BUILDERS:

1. *The Blind Side.* Directed by John Lee Hancock. 2009. Burbank, CA: Warner Bros., 2010. DVD.
2. Tenth Avenue North. "Strong Enough To Save," as recorded in *The Light Meets The Dark*. Nashville: Reunion Records, 2010.
3. Park, Andy. "We Will Ride," as recorded on *Change My Heart, O God*. Nashville: Starsong/EMD, 1997.

ADDITIONAL STUDY:

1. Kay, Ellie. *Heroes at Home: Help & Hope for America's Military Families.* Bloomington, MN: Bethany House, 2002.
2. Lucado, Max. 3:16: *The Numbers of Hope.* Nashville: Thomas Nelson, 2007.
3. Mansfield, Stephen. *The Faith of the American Soldier.* New York: Jeremy P. Tarcher / Penguin, 2005.

Acknowledgements

My wise grandmother used to tell us, "Many hands make light work."

I am very appreciative of the many hands that have made this *Resilience God Style* project such a fun and affirming venture.

For starters, my beloved wife Kathleen has been the calm influence behind the scenes, consistently sacrificing time and energy to create a work of value to others. Still waters run deep, and her wise insights along the way were invaluable. As my bride for 45 years, she has been a wonderful life partner, mother, grandmother, and friend to many. She has modeled resilience many times over, such as moving us 23 times in 31 years during our military service. She no doubt learned this from her highly resilient father and mother, Charlie and Bobbie Sue Robinson, who became my greatest cheerleaders over many life endeavors.

Another source of wisdom, encouragement, and tangible assistance has been our dear circle of "911 friends" and family, role models and wise counselors such as: Drs. Andy and Gail Seidel, Dr. Jim and Mary Syvrud, Bobby and Kandy Farino, Ron and Cristy Varela, Senior Pastor Bill and Lindy Warrick, Jeff and Karen Koob, Dr. Colonel (Chaplain) Ron Huggler and Colonel Sue Huggler, U.S. Army, Retired, Dr. Eric and Donna Scalise, Dr. LuAnn Callaway, Ben and Nancy Manthei, Paul and Betty Lou Martin, Chuck and Sharron Allen, Brigadier General Art and Cheryl Dillon, U.S. Army, Retired, Charles and Nancy Robinson, and our beloved children, Lieutenant Colonel Rob Dees and Allison Dees Barry, along with their respective families.

Our small group Bible study from Williamsburg Community Chapel was essential, participating in a ten-week pilot of the resilience concepts contained in *Resilient Warriors,* the precursor to this *Resilience God Style* book. These fellow resilient warriors provided valuable insights and continual encouragement to stay the course. This small band of brothers and sisters included Bobby and Kandy Farino, Jeff and Karen Koob, Jeff and Kim McManigal, Dr. Sharni and Dorothy Rakhra, Scott and Amanda MacLeod, Sam and Shannon Meyyar, Jason and Julie Farino, Randi and Gene Frazier, and Ronnie Vaught. Their commitment to this project will surely have impact far beyond the bounds of our small group, extending to many around our nation and our world.

Over the past seven years following publication of *Resilient Warriors,* many individuals and groups have provided insights regarding refinement of the *Resilience God Style* theme. Many churches, Christian men's organizations, veterans groups, and thousands of Liberty University students have affirmed this resilience content, and painted their own life experiences into the rich fabric of resilience profiles. This input has not only validated the content of this book, but has also provided stimulus to the forthcoming *Resilience God Style Video Series* and *Resilience God Style Training Game*. I am grateful to these fellow warriors who have added their expertise and experience to this "united effort of many."

My utmost respect and appreciation also goes to the brave ones who have shared their stories of pain, recovery, and resilience: Gary and Lolly Beikirch, Robert and Amy Nuttall, Scotty and Tiffany Smiley, Allen Clark, Phil Downer and family, Lacie Habekott, Nate and Julie Self, Deacon and Sharon Collins, Dr. LuAnn Callaway and Jacob Callaway, and Sergeant Merlin German, USMC, Retired.

Glen Aubrey of Creative Team Publishing (www.CreativeTeamPublishing.com) has been an outstanding editor, publisher, and friend. Justin Aubrey's artistic giftedness was indispensable to the cover designs. Randy Beck did a great job crafting our Resilience God Style website (including www.ResilienceGodStyle.com) and integrating social media into the effort. Jim Parroco and his team at Parroco Production Group have likewise been invaluable partners in the *Resilience God Style* project.

Foundational to my appreciation and understanding of resilience have been the inspiring Soldiers, Sailors, Airmen, Marines, and Guardsmen of our U.S. Armed Forces. They, along with their families, are true resilient warriors who inspire us daily. As well, our veterans of past military service constantly whisper strength, courage, and resilience through their legacy to our nation. Where would we be without them?

Most importantly, God truly is my Rock, Fortress, and Deliver ("RFD"). Without the friendship of Jesus, the comfort of His Holy Spirit, the wisdom of His Word, and the Sovereign and Sufficient Hand of God the Father, my efforts would only be clanging cymbals and tinkling brass. To Him Be the Glory!

About the Author
ROBERT F. DEES
Major General, U.S. Army, Retired

Major General (Retired) Robert F. Dees was born in Amarillo, Texas on 2 February 1950. Graduating from the US Military Academy in 1972, he was commissioned as a second lieutenant of Infantry and awarded a Bachelor of Science degree. He also holds a Masters degree in Operations Research from the Naval Postgraduate School. His military education includes the Infantry Officer Basic and Advanced Courses, the US Army Command and General Staff College, and the Industrial College of the Armed Forces. He was also a Research Fellow at the Royal College of Defence Studies in London and was licensed as a registered Professional Engineer in the State of Virginia.

General Dees served in a wide variety of command and staff positions culminating in his last three assignments as Assistant Division Commander for Operations, 101st Airborne Division (Air Assault); Commander, Second Infantry Division, United States Forces Korea; and as Deputy Commanding General, V (US/GE)

Corps in Europe, concurrently serving as Commander, US-Israeli Combined Task Force for Missile Defense. He commanded airborne, air assault, and mechanized infantry forces from platoon through division level; including two tours as company commander and regimental commander in the historic "Rakkasans," the 187th Regimental Combat Team. General Dees is a Distinguished Member of the Regiment, and has served a five-year tenure as Honorary Colonel of the Regiment for the Rakkasans.

General Dees' awards and decorations include the Defense Distinguished Service Medal, Distinguished Service Medal (2), Legion of Merit (2), Meritorious Service Medal (6), Joint Service Commendation Medal, Army Commendation Medal, and the Republic of Korea Chonsu Order of National Security. General Dees has also been awarded the Ranger Tab, Senior Parachutist and Air Assault Badges, the Expert Infantryman's Badge, the Army Staff Identification Badge, and the Joint Staff Identification Badge. General Dees was also awarded the 2003 Centurion Award by the National Association for Evangelicals for long term support to chaplains while in command positions.

Officially retiring from the Army on 1 January 2003, he worked as Director of Homeland Security for Electronic Warfare Associates; then as Executive Director, Defense Strategies, Microsoft Corporation for two years. In that role, General Dees formulated the strategy for Microsoft's US Defense sector and engaged with leadership of Microsoft's major defense partners. In addition, he served as Microsoft lead for Reconstruction of Iraq, coordinating efforts with US Government, foreign governments, and private sector partners in the US and abroad. General Dees then served for five years (2005-2010) as Executive Director, Military Ministry providing spiritual nurture to troops and families around the world. Following this General Dees served as Associate Vice President for Military Outreach for Liberty University (leading the Liberty University Institute for Military Resilience), Military Director for the American Association of Christian Counselors, and Senior Military Advisor for DNA Military. His Resilience Trilogy books (*Resilient Warriors*, *Resilient Leaders*, and *Resilient Nations*) are used in Psychology, Counseling, Business, Religion, and Government courses at Liberty University. He has also authored *Resilience God Style*, an associated *Resilience God Style Study Guide*, a *Resilience God Style Video Series*, and a *Resilience God Style Training Game.*

General Dees also served as National Security Advisor, followed by Presidential Campaign Chairman, for Dr. Ben Carson. He is now President of Resilience Consulting, LLC, serving a variety of constituents in the arenas of resilience consulting, business, cyber defense, counterterrorism, and care for military troops and families. As well, General Dees serves on the Board of Directors of the Lindell Foundation, bringing help, hope, and healing to addicts, downtrodden veterans, and other needy populations in America and beyond.

General Dees frequently provides leadership and resilience talks at a variety of seminars and conferences, as well as commentary on current military and resilience issues in venues such as FOX Huckabee, FOX Business, Council for National Policy, Focus on the Family, Christian Broadcasting Network, American Association of Christian Counselors, American Family Radio, Wildfire Men's Conferences, New Canaan Society, Pinnacle Forum, Wallbuilders Live, and numerous churches across America. He was featured as one of 30 "Master Leaders" by George Barna, and was presented the 2018 George Washington Military Leadership Award by the Council for National Policy.

General Dees is married to the former Kathleen Robinson of Houston, Texas. They have two married children and seven grandchildren, and are grateful for the privilege of continuing to serve God, Nation, and others during these critical times.

Permissions and Credits

In Order of Appearance:

Grateful acknowledgment is made to the following for permission to cite previously published material, quotes, and concepts:

David R. Segal and Mady Wechsler Segal, "America's Military Population," Population Bulletin 59, no. 4 (Washington, DC: Population Reference Bureau, 2004).

John Watson for quotes from Sun Tzu's Art of War, http://suntzusaid. com/book/3/18/. Copyright © 2011 John Watson, LLC. Reprinted by permission of John Watson.

Merriam-Webster for the definition of *resilience:* Used by permission. From *Merriam-Webster's Collegiate® Dictionary ©2011* by Merriam- Webster, Incorporated (www.Merriam-Webster.com).

Rich Tedeschi and his colleagues at The University of North Carolina at Charlotte for use of the term "seismic event" and excerpts from UNC Charlotte's webpage about Posttraumatic Growth:http://ptgi.uncc.edu/ whatisptg.htm. © 2003 UNC Charlotte. Page last updated 12 November 2010. Accessed 21 October 2011.

John Buckley for the excerpt from *National Association of Blind Teachers.* Found on http://www.blindteachers.net/west-point.html. Page last updated: unknown. Accessed 5 September 2011.

Science Progress for excerpts from Beryl Lieff Benderly's article, *Deciphering Today's Signature War Injury: Without More Knowledge, TBI and PTSD Are Ticking Time Bombs.* This material was first published by Science Progress. (http://www.scienceprogress.org)

Merriam-Webster for the definition of *calling:* Used by permission. From *Merriam-Webster's Collegiate® Dictionary ©2011* by Merriam-Webster, Incorporated (www.Merriam-Webster.com).

Daniel Webster Whittle: Text to "I Know Whom I Have Believed." Found in *Gospel Hymns Nos. 5 and 6 Combined.* Published by The Bigelow & Main Co. and The John Church Co. in 1892. Hymn lyrics are held within the public domain.

Tyndale House Publishers, Inc. for the excerpt taken from *TWO WARS* by Nate Self. Copyright © 2008 by Nate Self. Used by permission of Tyndale House Publishers, Inc. All rights reserved.

Mr. Walt Kelly, creator of the comic character *Pogo* and originator of the phrase *"We have met the enemy and he is us."*

John Donne: "No Man Is An Island" is held within the public domain.

Baseball-Almanac.com: Willie Mays' quote courtesy of Baseball Almanac. http://www.baseball-almanac.com/ Accessed 4 November 2011.

Archibald Signorelli: "If we yield to evil persuasions, it is because we fall the way we lean." Quote taken from *Plan of Creation, or Sword of Truth* by Archibald Signorelli. Published by Charles H. Kerr & Company in Chicago. © 1916. Book is held within the public domain.

Random House/Random House, Inc. for excerpts taken from *Unbroken*, © 2010 by Laura Hillenbrand. Used by permission of Random House, Inc., New York NY 10019. All rights reserved.

Dr. Bill Bright and Campus Crusade for Christ for use of the concept "Spiritual Breathing" as developed by Dr. Bright.

Zondervan for excerpts taken from *The Land Between* by Jeff Manion. Copyright © 2010 by Zondervan. Use by permission of Zondervan. http:// www.zondervan.com.

Zenith Press for excerpts taken from *Wounded Soldier, Healing Warrior,*©2007 Zenith Press, by Allen Clark. Reprinted by permission of Zenith Press, part of the Quayside Publishing Group, Minneapolis, MN 55401. All rights reserved.

Eternal Impact Publishing for excerpts taken from *From Hell To Eternity,*©2010 Eternal Impact Publishing, by Phil Downer. Reprinted by permission of Eternal Impact Publishing, Signal Mountain, TN 37377. All rights reserved.

John Bevere, *The Bait of Satan* (Lake Mary, FL: Charisma House, 2004). Used by permission.

Thomas Nelson, Inc. for excerpts taken from Sharon Hart May's contribution to *Caring for People God's Way: Personal and Emotional Issues, Addictions, Grief and Trauma*, © 2005, edited by Tim Clinton, Archibald Hart and George Ohlschlager. Reprinted with permission of Thomas Nelson, Inc., Nashville TN 37214. All rights reserved.

Maranatha! Music: Five stages of healing from grief. On the CD *An Invitation to Comfort: A Healing Journey Through Grief.*

Grateful Acknowledgement
is made to the following for permission to
publish their personal stories.

In Order of Appearance:

Chaplain (Major General) Doug Carver, U.S. Army, Retired, former Army Chief of Chaplains

Major Robert Nuttall, U.S. Army, Retired (and wife Amy)

Dr. LuAnn Callaway, professional counselor; and son Jacob, former Georgia National Guard infantryman

Gary Beikirch, former Special Forces Medic, and Medal of Honor, Vietnam (and wife Lolly)

Dr. Jerry White, former Air Force Major General and International President Emeritus of the Navigators

Grateful Acknowledgement

Captain Scotty Smiley, U.S. Army (and wife Tiffany)

General David Petraeus, U.S. Army, Retired, current Director of Central Intelligence Agency

Nate Self, former Army Ranger and Infantry Captain (and wife Julie)

Lieutenant Colonels Sharon and Deacon Collins, U.S. Army, Retired, Gold Star Parents

The Honorable Allen Clark, Vietnam Veteran and former Assistant Secretary of Veterans Affairs

Phil Downer, Vietnam Veteran and President of Discipleship Network of America

Lacie Habekott, Dallas Theological Seminary Graduate and missionary to the military

Index

Bibliography

Adsit, Chris. *The Combat Trauma Healing Manual: Christ-centered Solutions for Combat Trauma.* Newport News, VA: Military Ministry, 2007.

Adsit, Chris, Rahnella Adsit and Marshéle Carter Waddell. *When War Comes Home: Christ-Centered Healing for Wives of Combat Veterans.* Newport News, VA: Military Ministry, 2008.

Alexander, Eric. *The Summit: Faith Beyond Everest's Death Zone.* Green Forest, AR: New Leaf, 2010.

Alley, Lee. *Back From War: Finding Hope & Understanding in Life After Combat.* With assistance from Wade Stevenson. Midlothian, VA: Exceptional, 2007.

Ambrose, Stephen. *Undaunted Courage: Meriwether Lewis, Thomas Jefferson and the Opening of the American West.* New York: Simon & Schuster, 2003.

American Bible Society. *God Understands When You Fear Death.* God Understands Series. 8 vols. (unnumbered). New York: American Bible Society, 2009.

American Bible Society. *God Understands When You Feel Angry.* God Understands Series. 8 vols. (unnumbered). New York: American Bible Society, 2009.

American Bible Society. *God Understands When You Feel Hopelessness and Despair.* God Understands Series. 8 vols. (unnumbered). New York: American Bible Society, 2009.

American Bible Society. *God Understands When You Feel Life Is Meaningless and Without Purpose.* God Understands Series. 8 vols. (unnumbered). New York: American Bible Society, 2009.

American Bible Society. *God Understands When You Feel Life Is Unfair.* God Understands Series. 8 vols. (unnumbered). New York: American Bible Society, 2009.

American Bible Society. *God Understands When You Feel Overwhelmed With Guilt.* God Understands Series. 8 vols. (unnumbered). New York: American Bible Society, 2009.

American Bible Society. *God Understands When You Feel Sadness and Grief.* God Understands Series. 8 vols. (unnumbered). New York: American Bible Society, 2009.

American Bible Society. *God Understands When You Have Doubts.* God Understands Series. 8 vols. (unnumbered). New York: American Bible Society, 2009.

Amos Jr., James H. *The Memorial: A Novel of the Vietnam War.* Lincoln, NE: iUniverse.com, 2001.

Antal, John. *Hell's Highway: The True Story of the 101st Airborne Division During Operation Market Garden, September 17-25, 1944.* Minneapolis: Zenith, 2008.

Archer, Bernice and Kent Fedorowich. "The Women of Stanley: internment in Hong Kong, 1942-45." *Women's History Review* 5, no. 3 (1996): 373-399.

Barclay, William, trans. *The Letters to the Corinthians.* Revised ed. Philadelphia: Westminster, 1975. First published 1954 by The Saint Andrew Press in Edinburgh, Scotland.

———, trans. *The Letters to the Galatians and Ephesians.* Philadelphia: Westminster, 1976. First published 1954 by The Saint Andrew Press in Edinburgh, Scotland.

Barton, Ruth Haley. *Strengthening the Soul of Your Leadership: Seeking God in the Crucible of Ministry.* Downers Grove, IL: InterVarsity Press / IVP Books, 2008.

Benderly, Beryl Lieff. "Deciphering Today's Signature War Injury: Without More Knowledge, TBI and PTSD Are Ticking Time Bombs." *Science Progress.* Last modified December 2, 2008. http://scienceprogress.org/2008/12/deciphering-todays-signature-war-injury/.

Bevere, John. *The Bait of Satan.* 10th Anniversary Ed. Lake Mary, FL: Charisma House, 2004.

Bonhoeffer, Dietrich. *The Cost of Discipleship.* New York: Touchstone, 1995.

———. *Letters & Papers From Prison, The Enlarged Edition*. Edited by Eberhard Bethge. New York: Touchstone, 1997.

Bradley, James. *Flags of Our Fathers*. New York: Bantam Dell, 2000.

Brinsfield, John W., William C. Davis, Benedict Maryniak and James I. Robertson, Jr., eds. *Faith in the Fight: Civil War Chaplains.* Mechanicsburg, PA: Stackpole Books, 2003.

Buck, Janie and Mary Lou Davis. *Flight Path: A Biography of Frank Barker Jr.* Scotland, UK: Christian Focus, 2003.

Cantrell, Bridget C. and Chuck Dean. *Down Range to Iraq and Back.* Seattle: WordSmith, 2005.

Cash, Carey H. *A Table in the Presence*. Nashville: W Publishing Group, 2004.

Charles, J. Daryl and Timothy J. Demy. *War, Peace and Christianity: Questions and Answers from a Just-War Perspective*. Wheaton, IL: Crossway, 2010.

Clark, Allen. *Wounded Soldier, Healing Warrior: A Personal Story of a Vietnam Veteran Who Lost His Legs but Found His Soul*. St. Paul, MN: Zenith, 2007.

Clinton, Tim, Archibald Hart and George Ohlschlager, eds. *Caring for People God's Way: Personal and Emotional Issues, Addictions, Grief and Trauma*. Nashville: Thomas Nelson / Nelson Reference & Electronic, 2005.

Clinton, Tim and Ron Hawkins, eds. *The Popular Encyclopedia of Christian Counseling*. Eugene, OR: Harvest House, 2011.

Cook, Jane Hampton, Jocelyn Green and John Croushorn. *Battlefields & Blessings: Stories of Faith and Courage from the War in Iraq & Afghanistan*. Chattanooga, TN: God & Country, 2009.

Coy, Colonel Jimmie Dean. *A Gathering of Eagles*. 2nd ed. Mobile, AL: Evergreen, 2004.

———. *Prisoners of Hope: A Gathering of Eagles, Book Three*. Mobile, AL: Evergreen, 2005.

———. *Valor: A Gathering of Eagles.* Mobile, AL: Evergreen, 2003.

Dees, Robert F. *Resilient Warriors*. San Diego, CA: Creative Team Publishing, 2011.

———. *Resilient Warriors Advanced Study Guide*. San Diego, CA: Creative Team Publishing, 2012.

———. *Resilient Leaders*. San Diego, CA: Creative Team Publishing, 2013.

———. *Resilient Nations*. San Diego, CA: Creative Team Publishing, 2014.

———. *Resilience God Style Study Guide*. Ft. Worth, TX. Creative Team Publishing, 2018.

DeMoss, Nancy Leigh. *Choosing Forgiveness: Your Journey to Freedom.* Chicago: Moody, 2006.

———. *Choosing Gratitude: Your Journey to Joy.* Chicago: Moody, 2009.

Downer, Phil. *From Hell To Eternity: Life After Trauma.* Signal Mountain, TN: Eternal Impact, 2010.

"Empire Discontinued." *The Economist Newspaper Limited.* June 5, 2003. Accessed November 7, 2011. http://www.economist.com/node/1825845?story_id=1825845

Gražulis, Nijolé, trans. & ed. *The Chronicle of the Catholic Church in Lithuania,* Vol. 1. Chicago: Loyola University Press and Society for the Publication of the Chronicle of the Catholic Church in Lithuania, 1981.

———. *The Chronicle of the Catholic Church in Lithuania, V*ol. 6. Chicago: Society of the Chronicle of Lithuania, 1989.

Hedrick, David T. and Gordon Barry Davis, Jr. *I'm Surrounded by Methodists: Diary of John H. W. Stuckenberg. . . .* Gettysburg, PA: Thomas, 1995.

Hill, Margaret, Harriet Hill, Richard Bagge and Pat Miersma. *Healing the Wounds of Trauma: How the Church Can Help.* Nairobi, Kenya: Paulines Publications Africa, 2004.

Hillenbrand, Laura. *Unbroken.* New York: Random House, 2010.

Hurt, Bruce. "Romans 5:3 Commentary." P-R-E-C-E-P-T A-U-S-T-I-N. Last modified January 1, 2011. http://www.preceptaustin.org/romans_53-5.htm.

Hutchens, James M. *Beyond Combat.* Great Falls, VA: The Shepherd's Press, 1986.

Bibliography

Jackson Jr., Harry R. *The Warrior's Heart: Rules of Engagement for the Spiritual War Zone*. Grand Rapids: Chosen Books, 2004.

Jones, J. William. *Christ in the Camp: The True Story of the Great Revival During the War Between the States.* Harrisonburg, VA: Sprinkle, 1986.

Jordan, Merle R. "A Spiritual Perspective On Trauma and Treatment." *National Center for PTSD Clinical Quarterly* 5, no. 1, (Winter 1995): 9-10.

Kay, Ellie. *Heroes at Home: Help & Hope for America's Military Families.* Bloomington, MN: Bethany House, 2002.

Koenig, Harold G. *The Healing Power of Faith: How Belief and Prayer Can Help You Triumph Over Disease.* New York: Touchstone, 2001.

Kushner, Harold. *When Bad Things Happen to Good People.* New York: Anchor Books, 2004.

Lewis, C. S. *The Problem of Pain*. New York: Harper Collins, 2001. First published 1944 by Macmillan.

Light University. *Stress & Trauma Care: With Military Application.* Forest, VA: Light University, 2009. Counseling Certificate Training Program. DVD series. http://www.lightuniversity.com

Light University. *Stress & Trauma Care: With Military Application.* Forest, VA: Light University, 2009. Counseling Certificate Training Program. Workbook. http://www.lightuniversity.com

Lowney, Chris. *Heroic Leadership*. Chicago: Loyola, 2003.

Lucado, Max. *3:16: The Numbers of Hope*. Nashville: Thomas Nelson, 2007.

Lueders, Beth J. *Lifting Our Eyes: Finding God's Grace Through the Virginia Tech Tragedy; The Lauren McCain Story*. New York: Berkeley Books, 2007.

Luttrell, Marcus. *Lone Survivor: The Eyewitness Account of Operation Redwing and the Lost Heroes of Seal Team 10.* With the assistance of Patrick Robinson. New York: Little, Brown, 2007.

MacArthur, John. *The MacArthur New Testament Commentary: Romans 1-8.* Chicago: Moody, 1991.

MacDonald, Gordon. *Mid-Course Correction: Re-Ordering Your Private World for the Next Part of Your Journey.* Nashville: Thomas Nelson, 2005.

Manion, Jeff. *The Land Between: Finding God in Difficult Times.* Grand Rapids: Zondervan, 2010.

Mansfield, Stephen. *The Faith of the American Soldier*. New York: Jeremy P. Tarcher / Penguin, 2005.

Maranatha! Music. *An Invitation to Comfort: A Healing Journey Through Grief.* Narrated by Dr. Tim Clinton. Nashville: Maranatha! Music, 2008. CD.

"Medal of Honor Recipients: Vietnam (A—L)." *U.S. Army Center of Military History.* Last modified November 18, 2011. http://www.history.army.mil/html/moh/vietnam-a-l.html.

Military Ministry. *Spiritual Fitness Handbook: A Christian Perspective for Soldiers & Families.* U.S. Army ed. Newport News, VA: Military Ministry, 2010.

Miller, Chuck. *The Spiritual Formation of Leaders: Integrating Spiritual Formation and Leadership Development.* N.p.: Xulon, 2007.

Morgan, Robert J. *Then Sings My Soul: 150 of the World's Greatest Hymn Stories.* Nashville: Thomas Nelson, 2003.

Mumford, Nigel W. D. and Caroline Temple. *Hand to Hand: From Combat to Healing.* Revised ed. New York: Church, 2006.

Phillips, Michael M. *The Gift of Valor: A War Story.* New York: Broadway Books, 2005.

Pizzo, Angelo. *Rudy.* Directed by David Anspaugh. Produced by Robert N. Fried and Cary Woods. Videocassette (VHS), 112 min. Burbank, CA: Columbia Tristar Home Video, 1993.

Plekenpol, Chris. *Faith in the Fog of War*. Sisters, OR: Multnomah, 2006.

"Posttraumatic Growth: A Brief Overview." UNC Charlotte. Accessed October 27, 2011. http://ptgi.uncc.edu/whatisptg.htm.

Rayburn, Robert G. *Fight the Good Fight: Lessons From the Korean War.* Lookout Mountain, TN: Covenant College Press, 1956.

Ruth, Peggy Joyce. *Psalm 91: God's Shield of Protection*. Military ed. Kirkwood, MO: Impact Christian Books, 2005.

Schaeffer, Edith. *Affliction: A Compassionate Look at the Reality of Pain and Suffering.* Grand Rapids: Baker Books, 1993.

Schaeffer, Francis A. *Joshua and the Flow of Biblical History.* Downers Grove, IL: InterVarsity Press, 1977.

Schiffer, Michael. *Lean On Me.* Directed by John G. Avildsen. Produced by Norman Twain. Videocassette (VHS), 109 min. Burbank, CA: Warner Bros., 1989.

Schumacher, John W. *A Soldier of God Remembers: Memoir Highlights of A Career Army Chaplain.* Nappanee, IN: Evangel, 2000.

Secretariat. Directed by Randall Wallace. 2010. Burbank, CA: Walt Disney Studios Home Entertainment. DVD.

Segal, David R. and Mady Wechsler Segal. "America's Military Population." *Population Bulletin* 59, no. 4 (Washington, DC: Population Reference Bureau, 2004).

Self, Nate. *Two Wars: One Hero's Fight on Two Fronts—Abroad and Within.* Carol Stream, IL: Tyndale House, 2008.

Shealy, Keith. *Letters from the Front*. Yorktown, VA: Eagle Project, 2007.

Shephard, Ben. *A War of Nerves: Soldiers and Psychiatrists in the Twentieth Century.* Cambridge: Harvard University Press, 2001.

Shive, Dave. *Night Shift: God Works in the Dark Hours of Life.* Lincoln, NE: Back to the Bible, 2001.

Signorelli, Archibald. *Plan of Creation or Sword of Truth.* Chicago: Charles H Kerr & Company, 1916.

Smiley, Scotty. *Hope Unseen: The Story of the U.S. Army's First Blind Active-Duty Officer.* With Doug Crandall. New York: Howard Books, 2010.

Sorge, Bob. *Pain Perplexity and Promotion: A Prophetic Interpretation of the Book of Job.* Grandview, MO: Oasis House, 1999.

Stanley, Charles. *How to Handle Adversity.* Nashville: Thomas Nelson, 1989.

Stowell, Joseph, M. *The Upside of Down: Finding Hope When It Hurts.* Grand Rapids: Discovery House, 2006.

Swenson, Richard. *Margin: Restoring Emotional, Physical, Financial, and Time Reserves to Overloaded Lives.* Colorado Springs: NavPress, 2004.

Tedeschi, Richard G. and Lawrence G. Calhoun. "Posttraumatic Growth: Conceptual Foundations and Empirical Evidence." *Psychological Inquiry* 15, no. 1 (2004): 1-18.

Ten Boom, Corrie. *The Hiding Place.* 35th Anniversary Ed. With Elizabeth and John Sherrill. Grand Rapids, MI: Chosen Books, 2006.

The Blind Side. Directed by John Lee Hancock. 2009. Burbank, CA: Warner Bros., 2010. DVD.
The War Within: Finding Hope for Post-Traumatic Stress. 2010. Grand Rapids: Discovery House, 2010. DVD.

Tribus, Paul. *The Scars of War.* Seattle: WordSmith, 2005.

Vanauken, Sheldon. *A Severe Mercy.* New York: Bantam Books, 1977.

Vine, W. E. *An Expository Dictionary of New Testament Words With Their Precise Meanings for English Readers.* Old Tappan, NJ: Fleming H. Revell, 1966 First published 1940.

White, Jerry. *The Joseph Road: Choices That Determine Your Destiny.* Colorado Springs: NavPress, 2010.

Willey, Barry E. *Out of the Valley.* Ft. Worth, TX: Creative Team Publishing, 2016.

Yancey, Philip. *Where Is God When It Hurts?* Grand Rapids: Zondervan, 1977.

Young, Sarah. *Jesus Calling: Enjoying Peace in His Presence.* Nashville: Thomas Nelson, 2004.

APPENDIX

Products and Services
Books, Video Series, Training Game

RESILIENCE GOD STYLE
ISBN: 978-0-9979519-2-9

RESILIENCE GOD STYLE STUDY GUIDE
ISBN: 978-0-9979519-3-6

RESILIENCE GOD STYLE VIDEO SERIES
See page 274

RESILIENCE GOD STYLE TRAINING GAME
See page 275

RESILIENT WARRIORS
ISBN: 978-0-9838919-4-9

RESILIENT WARRIORS ADVANCED STUDY GUIDE
ISBN: 978-0-9838919-5-6

RESILIENT LEADERS
ISBN: 978-0-9855979-9-3

RESILIENT NATIONS
ISBN: 978-0-9897975-6-6

FOR INFORMATION, COMMENTS, and QUESTIONS:

contact@ResilienceGodStyle.com

FOR SUPPORTING RESILIENCE CONTENT:

www.ResilienceGodStyle.com
See "Resources" tab for worksheets and presentations

Facebook: Resilience God Style

Twitter: @GodBounce

Instagram: Resilience God Style

Resilience Consulting LLC
1801 Red Bud Lane
Suite B-298
Round Rock, Texas 78664

*****

CPSIA information can be obtained
at www.ICGtesting.com
Printed in the USA
JSHW081538090323
38696JS00004B/13